ADDING ON

Other Publications:
SUCCESSFUL PARENTING
HEALTHY HOME COOKING
UNDERSTANDING COMPUTERS
YOUR HOME
THE ENCHANTED WORLD
THE KODAK LIBRARY OF CREATIVE PHOTOGRAPHY
GREAT MEALS IN MINUTES
THE CIVIL WAR
PLANET EARTH
COLLECTOR'S LIBRARY OF THE CIVIL WAR
THE EPIC OF FLIGHT
THE GOOD COOK
WORLD WAR II
THE OLD WEST

For information on and a full description of any of the Time-
Life Books series listed above, please write:

   Reader Information
   Time-Life Books
   541 North Fairbanks Court
   Chicago, Illinois 60611

This volume is part of a series offering homeowners
detailed instructions on repairs, construction
and improvements they can undertake themselves.

HOME REPAIR
AND IMPROVEMENT

ADDING ON

BY THE EDITORS OF
TIME-LIFE BOOKS

TIME-LIFE BOOKS,
ALEXANDRIA, VIRGINIA

HOME REPAIR AND IMPROVEMENT

Editorial Staff for Adding On

Editor	William Frankel
Assistant Editor	Lee Hassig
Designer	Kenneth E. Hancock
Picture Editor	Adrian Allen
Associate Designer	Lorraine D. Rivard
Text Editors	Russell B. Adams Jr., David Thiemann
Staff Writers	Lynn R. Addison, William C. Banks, Megan Barnett, Stephen Brown, Malachy Duffy, Richard Flanagan, Steven J. Forbis, Geoffrey B. Henning, Bonnie Bohling Kreitler, Leslie Marshall, Brooke Stoddard, William Worsely
Art Associates	George Bell, Elizabeth Reed, Richard Whiting
Art Coordinator	Anne B. Landry
Copy Coordinators	Margery duMond, Brian Miller
Editorial Assistant	Susan S. Trice

Editorial Operations

Copy Chief	Diane Ullius
Editorial Operations	Caroline A. Boubin (manager)
Production	Celia Beattie
Quality Control	James J. Cox (director)
Library	Louise D. Forstall

Correspondents: Elisabeth Kraemer-Singh (Bonn); Dorothy Bacon (London); Maria Vincenza Aloisi (Paris); Ann Natanson (Rome). Valuable assistance was also provided by: Judy Aspinall, Karin B. Pearce (London); Carolyn T. Chubet, Miriam Hsia, Christina Lieberman (New York); Mimi Murphy (Rome).

THE CONSULTANTS: Louis Genuario, a general contractor in northern Virginia, specializes in remodeling and additions. He has studied engineering at West Point and Harvard.

Harry H. Herman Jr. is an independent consulting engineer to government and industry with a special interest in single-family houses. President of his own consulting firm in Washington, D.C., Mr. Herman has won awards for engineering excellence and holds several patents.

Thomas L. Kerns is an architect based in Washington, D.C. His firm has won local and national awards for residential design.

Roswell W. Ard is a consulting structural engineer and a professional home inspector in northern Michigan. He has written professional papers on wood-frame construction techniques.

Harris Mitchell, a special consultant for Canada, has worked in the field of home repair and improvement for more than two decades. He is Homes editor of *Today* magazine and author of a syndicated newspaper column, "You Wanted to Know," as well as a number of books on home improvement.

Time-Life Books Inc. offers a wide range of fine recordings, including a *Rock 'n' Roll Era* series. For subscription information, call 1-800-621-7026 or write Time-Life Music, P.O. Box C-32068, Richmond, Virginia 23261-2068.

Library of Congress Cataloguing in Publication Data

Time-Life Books.
  Adding On
  (Home repair and improvement, v. 17)
  Includes index.
  1. Dwellings — Remodeling. I. Title.
TH4816.T55 1979   643'.7   79-9759
ISBN 0-8094-2416-9
ISBN 0-8094-2415-0 lib. bdg.
ISBN 0-8094-2414-2 retail ed.

Contents

Before Building Begins

Laying the groundwork. **Laying the groundwork.** From the photograph of his modest house, a homeowner made a rough scale drawing of an extension that increased the floor space by 40 per cent but preserved the architectural integrity of the original. In turn, the sketch served as the basis for the more precise plans (pages 16-17) that must be submitted with an application for a building permit—and with the permit in hand, the amateur builder had official approval to go to work.

The idea has fascinated kings and commoners: adding new space to an existing home can increase enjoyment inside and beauty outside. You do not have to be Louis XIV, who expanded his father's hunting lodge at Versailles to accommodate 5,000 people, or even Thomas Jefferson, who shaped and reshaped a cottage at Monticello for 40 years, to conceive and construct a handsome, useful expansion of your house. Before building begins, there are choices to weigh and challenges to assess.

Whatever your need—a breakfast nook, new bedrooms and baths, a family room or extra space in a living room—there are three possible ways to achieve it: building out, by adding a small extension alongside an exterior wall; building up, by placing a second story atop an attached garage or installing a dormer in an attic; or building in any direction to create a major addition, a collection of rooms that forms an independent wing of the house.

All additions have one characteristic in common—at the junction of the new and the old, strange metamorphoses occur. Outside walls turn into inside ones, roofs turn into supports and ceilings turn into weight-bearing floors. Crucial to the chemistry of such changes is splicing the new to the old. It is the techniques required for these connections—rather than the basics of trades work or the job of finishing an addition's exterior and interior—that this book concentrates on. Cantilevered joists, for example, tie the floor of a walk-in bay window to the house floor. Extra studs are integrated into existing walls to mate with the ends of new ones. A weathertight joint between a new roof and the old depends on precise measuring and marking, cutting and joining.

An addition raises an important esthetic challenge: creating architectural harmony between the old and the new. Although there are a few time-honored guidelines for matching an addition to a house (pages 8-15), you are likely to find an architect's advice helpful in solving esthetic problems. But whether you use a professional's experience or your own good taste, the result should be an addition that looks as if it ought to have been there all along.

The Basic Skills

This volume concentrates on the special techniques of constructing an addition and joining it to a main house. The reader is assumed to be familiar with the basic skills involved in masonry, plumbing, wiring, roofing and siding. Detailed introductions to the techniques of those crafts are contained in other volumes in the HOME REPAIR AND IMPROVEMENT series.

The Art of Making an Addition Look Right

An ugly addition is a bad bargain. It ruins the architecture of a house, antagonizes neighbors and may reduce the value of your property; worse still, it often proves difficult to live in. But properly designed, an addition enhances a house, as the drawings on these pages and the photographs on pages 49 through 55 show.

Achieving the proper design for an addition requires the talents of a good architect. If you possess them, you may want to create your own design. But most people rely on a professional. You can hire an architect—either for a prearranged sum (generally about 11 per cent of a contractor's estimated cost for the addition) or an hourly rate. The architect will supervise the job for an additional 4 per cent of the estimated cost, but most do-it-yourself builders dispense with this service. If you need advice later, you can pay an hourly fee for it.

An architect will provide drawings that you will need to obtain building permits. If you prepare the design yourself, you can still hire a draftsman to prepare working drawings or make the drawings yourself; most building departments accept fairly rough sketches (pages 16-17).

Regardless of who designs the addition, the first step is to prepare what architects call a program, listing the use and approximate dimensions of each new room. Rectangular rooms, approximately half again as long as they are wide, are generally most comfortable. For the best light and ventilation, locate windows on two walls; try to place doors near corners to provide more unbroken wall space for chairs and tables. Also consider how each room should relate to surrounding ones, with an eye toward problems with noise, access and light: a noisy family room should not be next to a bedroom, for example. Where possible, illustrate your program with photographs, magazine clippings and sketches.

Site conditions, zoning ordinances and your space requirements together will determine which of three options you will pursue: building out horizontally from the house, building up above it or building a major addition—a two-story wing, perhaps, or a full second story. Each set of drawings on these pages shows how a particular type of addi-tion—a bay window (opposite), for example—can be adapted to fit houses of several architectural styles. The drawings are not exhaustive; the techniques in this book apply to any type of addition and the additions shown here can be adapted to other architectural styles.

Theoretically, any style of addition can be made to look attractive on any style of house. All-glass modern wings have been grafted onto fussy Victorian structures with success—by architectural geniuses. But most designers play safe by following two simple rules. First, the architecture of the addition should echo that of the original house wherever possible. Ideally, the addition should mimic the house so well that you cannot tell where one stops and the other begins. The second rule applies when the addition must depart from the style of the house: the departure should be clear and intentional, in subdued contrast to the original. An inexact imitation may seem a mistake. These rules apply to all structural elements of the addition.

Three elements are particularly important: roof, windows and siding. The roof of an addition is seldom as high as an existing roof—the difference adds pleasing variety. The addition roof need not even be the same style as the house roof. Most houses have straight gable or hip roofs; a shed-roofed addition to either is a traditional style. However, adding a hip-roofed addition to a gable-roofed house or vice versa calls for discretion; either combination can look awkward unless carefully integrated.

The aspects of the roof that are crucial to appearance are details: slope, overhang and covering. The best-looking additions generally have roofs that match those of their existing houses in all three details. The principal exception to this rule is the addition with a shed roof. If the addition is not very deep, limiting the size of the roof, a very shallow slope often is used to contrast with the steep slope of the house roof.

In most cases, it is fairly simple to match roof slopes and—with some carpentry tricks (page 61)—overhangs. This is not true of the roof covering. While you usually can find roofing materials of the same size and shape as the ones you have, they almost never will match per-fectly. Generally you can settle for an approximate match, but if the roof is a dominant feature, you may want to re-roof the entire house.

Similar considerations must be taken into account for windows. If windows on an addition match those on the house in style—casements with casements, multi-paned double-hung types with their exact counterparts—the addition will be least obtrusive, although deliberate contrasts can be attractive.

More important than window style is position. Horizontal spacing often varies, although for the most pleasing appearance it should not seem random. The crucial aspect of window position is vertical alignment. If the tops of the windows do not line up, a distracting jagged line is introduced.

Siding generally is the simplest detail of an addition to match to the house. Many old-fashioned patterns still can be found in stock in lumberyards and, if necessary, you can order pieces specially milled to match at a fairly reasonable cost. In some cases you may not want to match the existing siding—combinations of shingles, clapboard, brick or vertical planking are traditional, although they can create a fussy effect on a small house or when several variations are used.

All these details combine to create the new look your addition gives to your home. In planning for this result, consider the effect inside on room layout and outside on what architects call the focus of the house—the point that naturally draws and holds your eye, such as the front door or a large window. Ideally, each side of the house has its own focus, but front and side views matter most. An addition may replace the original focus, but if it adds secondary focus—with its own striking shape, perhaps, or with a major feature like a sliding glass door—it confuses the design. Partly for this reason, most additions are built at the rear, leaving facades unchanged.

All these rules are overruled, of course, by gifted designers—the most strikingly beautiful additions achieve their impact because their builders dared to disregard convention. Individual taste must be the final authority. It is your house, and its addition must please you.

A bay window. The gently protruding bay window suits many styles. The stock unit, bought ready-made with a metal-roofing kit, is generally designed to adorn a traditional two-story colonial house *(bottom);* in this example the window is mounted on the side of the house, leaving the appearance of the façade unchanged. The same unit is doubled—one stacked on top of the other—to create the two-story bay typical of Victorian Gothic *(center),* even the curved windows of the upper bay can be ordered as part of a stock unit. To blend the addition with the original house, curved-shingle siding matches that on the original roof gable; the floor of each bay is supported by floor joists that are cantilevered from those in the original house.

For a modern ranch house *(top);* a simple bay can be assembled by building a shallow room extension from ordinary window units, 2-by-4 stud framing and a concrete-block foundation wall.

A new room. A modest addition outward—front, side or back—is the most common. To prevent the addition from looking like a bump on the house, it generally is given a roof that echoes the original. (Here and in some pictures following, the original lines of a house are indicated in gray.) On a split-level house (*top*), for example, an addition often duplicates the shape of the one-story portion. The two roofs have the same height and pitch and so meet naturally in valleys. The same approach works at the back or front of a ranch house (*center*). On a massive, boxy house, however, it is better to extend the original shape. For example, the walls and roof on one side of a colonial house (*bottom*) can be extended to create a classic salt-box shape, with a half-story of storage space opposite the second floor of the house. A clash of styles between old and new windows is averted by the distance between them and by the clear contrast of the large-scale simplicity of the new windows.

A wraparound addition. This design is particularly suited to two special types of houses: a small house, which would be overwhelmed by the mass of an ordinary addition; and a house on a lot so small that local setback requirements prohibit a large addition in one direction. For the colonial house at top, the addition roof is offset from the house roof but duplicates its width, pitch and soffit detail so well that the addition looks like a part of the house. On the Cape Cod (*lower drawing*), the front edge of the house roof has been extended with short rafters, and hips have been made from prefabricated trusses, creating a hip-on-gable roof that exactly matches the pitch of the original gable roof.

Extending an entire side. A shed-roofed addition that extends one end of a house suits almost any style of architecture. It is a traditional extension of American farmhouses and, because of its simplicity, adapts to such complicated styles as the Victorian or the Elizabethan (*above left*). A shed roof that is designed with a much shallower pitch than the original has a simple line that does not clash with the house roof or obstruct the second-story windows.

For the Elizabethan house, 1-inch boards applied over stucco or plywood siding match the original half-timbered style. On the large, boxy colonial at right, the full-side addition preserves the lines and massive look of the house.

Expanding Up—Unobtrusively

When the shape or terrain of a lot precludes building outward, building up—perhaps with a shed dormer *(below),* or a room above a garage *(opposite)*—often is the answer. This option introduces design problems of its own, however: second-floor additions have an unfortunate tendency to overwhelm the architecture of a house with their bulk.

To avoid obvious bulkiness, many upward additions are placed behind the house so that they do not obtrude on the view from the street. An alternative can serve if the second-story addition is at the side; in such a case you may be able to extend the house roof over the addition. And you sometimes can minimize the effect of the addition with an abundance of windows, which makes new construction look less massive. Horizontal panels of windows near the roof look best. To preserve symmetry, the spacing of old and new windows should match and the addition windows should be either centered between or located directly above first-floor doors and windows.

The floor plan of the addition will be determined largely by the location of the doorway or stairway that provides access to it. You may have to build a new stairway. For access to a shed dormer, the original attic stairs seldom meet building-code requirements; for access to a room over a garage, a doorway through the second-floor wall of the house often would route traffic through a bedroom. Try to place the lower landing of a new stairway in little-used space that opens off a hallway—a linen closet, perhaps, or the corner of the garage next to the house door—and place the upper landing in a corner of the addition.

A shed dormer. From the street, the dormer at the back of the colonial house at left below is hidden by the roof, the most common arrangement. On the Cape Cod house the dormer is located in front of the ridge, changing the façade; however, its design preserves the symmetry of the house by centering the two second-story windows between the original door and windows. The ceiling of this dormer is only 7 feet high because of the relatively low ridge of a small Cape Cod roof, but the large windows make it seem much higher. Both of them cover less than two thirds of the roof and stop short of the overhang, leaving a border of the original roofing to minimize their apparent size.

A room over the garage. If a garage originally was covered with a sun deck *(top)*, an addition can be erected directly on this platform, covered by a sideways extension of the house roof; the large windows play down the size of the addition. An addition on top of the garage of a one-story house *(middle)* needs a roof that matches the roof of the main house—in this case, an elaborate hip-on-gable roof over a capacious two-car garage makes the remodeled wing the largest, most prominent part of the house. An addition over a garage attached to a two-story house generally can be covered by extending a gable roof; in the example at bottom a hip diminishes the visual bulk of the addition.

How to Fit On a Large Addition

A massive expansion of a house, with a wing to one side *(opposite)* or a second floor added to the top of a one-story house *(below)*, introduces a series of interrelated practical and esthetic considerations. The traffic pattern inside is altered—perhaps forcing people to walk through the kitchen to get to a bathroom, or through a bedroom on the way to a patio. Hallways may be needed, at least 36 inches wide so that furniture can be moved easily and two people can pass without rubbing shoulders.

The floor plan probably will have to accommodate the posts, girders and bearing walls needed to support floor joists. Floors and walls must provide channels for plumbing pipes and heating ducts and may need to be reinforced to support heavy plumbing fixtures.

Expansion upward with a full second story disrupts life for the occupants, because the old roof generally must be removed. But building this type of addition, a job often left to professionals, offers a wide range of opportunities in design. While it is often possible simply to extend first-floor walls upward, matching the first-floor siding and window style, and to top them with a new roof that exactly matches the previous one, the massive addition also permits radical changes in style. So little is left of the original house that the designer has a relatively free hand, as the examples on these pages demonstrate.

A separate, two-story wing alters proportions radically, but because it leaves the original roof intact it generally is most attractive if it follows the style of the house closely. The result looks like the original, but bigger.

Unusual second stories. Rather than lift the roof to stretch an existing house, the planners of these two examples completely altered the original architecture with distinctive second stories. In the upper illustration, a conventional gable-roofed ranch house was doubled in size by building on top of it two overhanging gable-roofed wings—one for parents, one for children—that bracket a second-floor sun deck and are connected by a glassed-in breezeway. At bottom, a gambrel roof, assembled from a spiderweb of roof trusses to form sloping interior walls and a high "cathedral" ceiling, transforms one wing of what had been a typical L-shaped tract house.

A two-story wing. At top, a new section imitates the others of a half-timbered Elizabethan house that already had a variety of wings; the second story of the addition overhangs the first on cantilevered floor joists *(page 22)*, a typical feature of this style. The roof, siding and windows of the addition all match those on the existing structure. On the colonial at center, only the seam in the siding gives away the new wing, which is simply a sideways extension, stylistically identical, of the original. The hipped roof blends the shape of the addition with that of the house. The addition to the Victorian house at bottom extends a gable of the original roof, dividing the side of the house into three matched wings.

Planning the Job to Run Smoothly

Deciding what you want to build is just the first step in planning an addition. Another might be finding the labor to build it—some skilled homeowners handle the entire job themselves, others supplement their labor and talents with hired help.

Still another step is getting a plan of the addition onto paper. If an architect helps with the design of your addition, he will probably supply you with working drawings; otherwise, you must develop your own. These plans not only serve as a guide to construction; they also can be used to make a list of materials. After pricing materials for the jobs you will do yourself and soliciting bids on any other work, you can estimate the addition's cost—and seek financing for it.

The story of one family's project illustrates these preliminary steps.

The 17-by-22-foot addition to Bill and Leslie Stoddard's home in a suburb of Washington, D.C., is completely owner-built. Their decision to do everything, from the foundation piers to the finish molding, was based in part on an advantage that Bill Stoddard has over many amateur builders—he is retired. By providing their own labor, the Stoddards saved almost 50 per cent of what a contractor would have charged. And they were able to add custom touches that they would otherwise have foregone.

Bill regarded his addition, which took almost a year to complete, as something of a hobby, though Leslie admonishes, "It's not like needlepoint. You can't pick it up and put it down. Don't even start an addition unless you're willing to make it a major part of your life." As a rough rule of thumb, an amateur builder working evenings and weekends can estimate 3 hours per square foot of addition to finish the job, slightly more if he is unfamiliar with some of the tasks involved.

Obviously, a homeowner with less time than Bill Stoddard might prefer to act as a sort of general contractor, selecting the jobs he wants to do himself and hiring others to do the rest. If time is your major consideration, hire out the jobs that call for a high level of skill or specialized equipment; such jobs can eat up an amateur's time. Large concrete slabs, plastering, deep excavations and extensive grading fall into this category.

Simple Drawings for Official Approval

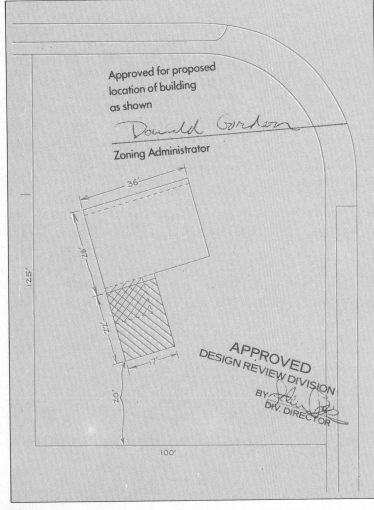

Approved for proposed location of building as shown

Donald Gordon

Zoning Administrator

36'

28'

22'

17'

20'

125'

100'

APPROVED
DESIGN REVIEW DIVISION
BY
DIV. DIRECTOR

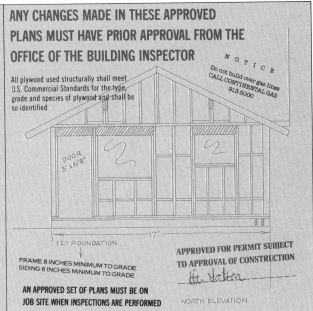

ANY CHANGES MADE IN THESE APPROVED PLANS MUST HAVE PRIOR APPROVAL FROM THE OFFICE OF THE BUILDING INSPECTOR

NOTICE

All plywood used structurally shall meet U.S. Commercial Standards for the type, grade and species of plywood and shall be so identified

Do not build over gas lines
CALL CONTINENTAL GAS
913-8000

DOOR 3' x 6'8"

12" FOUNDATION

17'

FRAME 8 INCHES MINIMUM TO GRADE
SIDING 6 INCHES MINIMUM TO GRADE

APPROVED FOR PERMIT SUBJECT TO APPROVAL OF CONSTRUCTION

AN APPROVED SET OF PLANS MUST BE ON JOB SITE WHEN INSPECTIONS ARE PERFORMED

NORTH ELEVATION

Two simple plans. Boldly stamped with building-department dos and don'ts, the plot plan (*left*) and elevation view (*above*) shown here were part of a set of drawings that Bill Stoddard used to estimate his materials costs, and later submitted with his application for a building permit. The shaded area of the plot plan shows the proposed location of his addition, at the back of the house over an old patio site, and gives its distance from the nearest property line. The elevation drawing shows an interior view of the addition's north wall as seen from the main house; similar drawings were submitted for the other walls.

If you like to do things with your hands but are bothered by working high above the ground, let someone else handle the siding and roofing jobs that take you more than 10 feet up. Work to be done deep underground is a special problem: excavations that go deeper than 4 feet down require professional shoring.

There are some jobs a professional can do more cheaply than you can. Because firms that install wallboard and shingles buy in large wholesale lots, they can often do a job for less than you would pay for the materials alone. Do small or complicated jobs yourself; leave large open surfaces that can be covered quickly to a subcontractor.

Bill Stoddard drew his own plans to scale and, since he planned to work on his own, he had no need to draw them so well that anyone else could use them. If you plan to hire others, draw precise plans and use the architectural symbols that are commonly understood by building tradespeople (below). Homeowner-drawn sketches generally are acceptable to building departments, lenders and subcontractors. For an hourly fee, an architect will check a homeowner's plans for important engineering details, such as the size and spacing of footings or the slope of a roof; if you wish, he will also render your rough drawings to scale, using standard symbols.

Bill estimated his materials costs by studying newspaper advertisements for the prices of the items he needed. You can also visit suppliers and write for manufacturer's retail price lists. The Stoddards needed only a materials estimate before they went for a loan. A homeowner planning to hire labor would need to get bids on labor and materials at this point.

Many home-improvement firms use their own contract forms when bidding. Modify these forms so they spell out your expectations about workmanship, materials and approximate schedules.

Schedules will be firmed up later, but the specifications covering workmanship and materials should be unmistakably clear from the start. Wall-finishing materials, for instance, should be described by type, thickness and method of finishing; windows, doors, faucets, lighting fixtures, and other equipment should be listed by manufacturer and model numbers.

A good contract leaves you with bargaining power if work or materials do not meet your requirements and gives you at least a year's guarantee on workmanship and materials. Specify that you will pay no more than 25 per cent of the total cost

The formal language of blueprints. Use these symbols, representing elements commonly included in an addition, when you render plans that will be used by others. All are readily recognized by building tradesmen and many, such as those for lavatories or doors, are obvious at a first glance. More abstract symbols, standing for such elements as switches or thermostats, are easy to decipher in the context of the floor plans, elevations and section views.

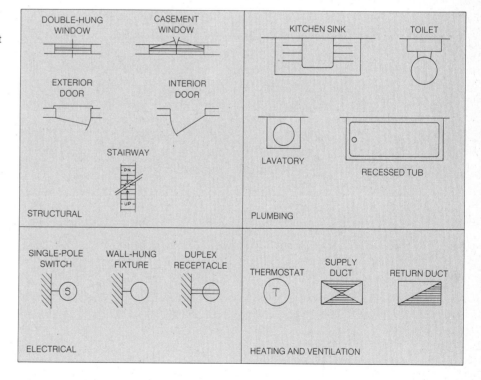

as a down payment, and that you will hold back at least 10 per cent until you have inspected the finished work and received waivers or receipts stating that the contractor has paid all suppliers and subcontractors.

Ask contractors or subcontractors to provide a certificate showing that they carry workmen's compensation and liability insurance. Otherwise, you must take out a workmen's compensation policy yourself and increase your own liability coverage through a separate policy or a change in your homeowner's insurance.

Your materials estimates and the bids from home-improvement firms will tell you whether you need financing. If you do, think of the money as one more element in your shopping list. Do not hesitate to bargain with bankers—interest rates and loan terms can be negotiable—

but remember that interest rates are only one factor in the total cost of a loan. The length of time you take to repay the loan, the institution's charges to write it, the cost of loan insurance, and the method of calculating interest all affect loan costs. Use all of this information in your comparison shopping for the best loan.

Before you sign a contract or buy materials, make a chronological checklist of all the jobs that must be done. The possibilities include excavating, laying a foundation, framing, masonry, plumbing, electrical work, heating and air-conditioning installations, insulation, putting up wallboard, painting, and finish-flooring. Add such steps as buying material for each job, applying for permits, scheduling subcontractors and calling—and waiting—for inspections.

For each job and step, estimate the

starting and completion dates. Add an allowance of at least two days per month for bad weather or unforeseen interruptions. Now you can set firm schedules and get under way.

With good paper planning, you should catch most mistakes before they are executed in concrete, studs and plywood. Those you miss should be minor, like those of the Stoddards. Bill Stoddard remembers that he underestimated the time-consuming drudgery of digging holes for his footings. "That Virginia clay was so tough that my son and I together couldn't turn more than three shovelfuls in fifteen minutes."

But he remembers, too, that most of the work went much as he planned it. "There was only one thing we really blew," he says, laughing. "We were way under on the beer estimate."

A Guide to Financing

Loan	Sources	Amount	Collateral or security
Insurance-policy loan	Insurance companies	Up to the cash value of a life insurance policy	The policy itself; if the borrower dies before the loan is repaid, the face value of the policy is reduced by the amount of the loan
Passbook loan	Some banks, most savings-and-loan associations (United States), trust companies (Canada), some credit unions	Up to the amount in a passbook account, certificates of deposit	Savings account or certificates
New mortgage on existing home	Most banks, savings-and-loan associations, trust companies; some credit unions, some finance companies	The cost of the addition plus the unpaid balance on the mortgage for your existing home	Existing home
Second mortgage on existing home	Most banks, savings-and-loan associations, trust companies, credit unions, finance companies	Usually up to 75 per cent of the amount of equity in existing home	Existing home
Home-improvement loans	Most banks, savings-and-loan associations, trust companies, credit unions, finance companies	Varying amounts based on borrower's credit standing, income and assets	Small loans sometimes not secured, larger amounts by existing home
FHA Title I loans	Banks, savings-and-loan associations, credit unions, finance companies approved by the Federal Housing Administration	Any amount up to a legally set maximum	Loans up to half the maximum amount not secured, larger amounts secured by existing home
Personal loans	Most banks, savings-and-loan associations, finance companies	Amount based on credit standing, income and assets	Unsecured

Shopping for financing. In this chart, the first column lists the types of loans available for financing an addition, ranked roughly in an ascending order of the interest rate over the life of a loan. The sources offering each type of loan are given in the second column; the third indicates the approximate limit on the amount of money you can borrow, and the fourth column describes the collateral or security generally required as a condition for obtaining the loan.

Scheduling Permits and Inspections

Inspection	When to call an inspector	Major checkpoints
Footing	After preparing the trenches, but before pouring concrete	Excavation, soil conditions, reinforcement
Backfill	After constructing the foundation walls and floor, but before backfilling	Walls, backfill material
Slab	After forms, gravel, vapor barriers, wire mesh or steel are in place, but before pouring concrete	Forms, soil condition, reinforcement
Rough plumbing	Underground plumbing: after installing pipes, but before filling trenches or pouring concrete Above-ground plumbing: after installing pipes, stacks, and vents in framing, but before walls are finished and fixtures installed	Stacks, vents, pipes
Rough electrical	After running cable and grounding boxes, but before walls are finished or electrical devices installed	Circuits, grounding
Framing	After plumbing and electrical rough-in work is approved, but before insulation or wall finish materials are installed	Sizes, spacing, holes, notches
Mechanical	After ductwork and insulation are installed, but before walls are finished and equipment installed	Ductwork and insulation surrounding it
Close-in	After installing all insulation materials, but before installing wall or ceiling finish materials	Insulation
Final plumbing, electrical, mechanical and building	After walls are finished and all plumbing, electrical and mechanical equipment and fixtures are installed and working, but before occupancy	Plumbing: fixtures and pipes watertight; electrical: outlets, switches and other devices operational; mechanical: ductwork unobstructed; building: structure weathertight, doors and windows in operation, grading completed

The right times for inspections. In most areas an addition must pass several inspections before it can receive a certificate of occupancy. The inspections are listed here in the sequence in which they normally occur; while not all of them will be required in every area, a building permit generally requires at least four inspections. These are an inspection of the foundation work, one of the framing, one after insulation is in, and a final inspection when all work is complete. The separate permits for electrical, plumbing, or heating or air-conditioning work commit you to inspections of the rough installation and the finished work. The second column in the chart indicates the point in the construction sequence when you must call in an inspector; the third lists the main features that will be checked for conformity to building codes.

Tips for Choosing a Contractor

There is no easy way of judging the skill and reliability of a home-improvement contractor or subcontractor, but you can check his past business dealings before you invest any money in his work.

Ask the local building department or licensing bureau whether the contractor or subcontractor has a trade license. States, Canadian provinces and some local jurisdictions license plumbers, electricians, air-conditioning and heating contractors and home-improvement or remodeling specialists. A licensed contractor or tradesman has passed a test proving his competence in his specialty and in some areas he must post a bond as insurance against bankruptcy or other default on his work.

Look through the building permits on file at the building department. Find jobs similar to yours, call the owners of the houses and ask about the contractor's work; for a more thorough check, ask for permission to inspect the jobs. If you already have a contractor in mind, check the permits for his jobs and call the owners for references and permission to see the work. Call the local Better Business Bureau or consumer protection agency to see if there have been complaints about the contractor. If there have been any at all, be wary.

Finally, ask the contractor several questions. Does he carry workmen's compensation and liability insurance? Will he give you lien waivers from suppliers and subcontractors, stating that they have been paid? Will a down payment of 25 per cent be adequate on large jobs? If the answer to any of these questions is no, keep shopping.

A new window on the world. A ready-made bay window—one of a variety of styles available—leans against a blank, somewhat forbidding wall. Installed on a short knee wall that sets the unit at the conventional height above the house floor, the triple window provides a simple way to add space to a house.

A ground-floor addition to the back, side or front of a house is by far the easiest to plan and build. You may need no more than a full-height bay window *(pages 22-35),* made with a factory unit fitted into the wall, to provide extra light and floor space. But any addition of modest size is relatively simple. Most of the work, from digging trenches for the new foundation to nailing the rafters to the walls, is done close to the ground. Because joists in small additions are commonly less than 15 feet long, they can usually be made of single lengths of lumber, saving the work of building piers and installing a support girder. Wall sections, too, are short and lightweight—a 10-foot section generally weighs no more than 110 pounds, and with the aid of a helper or two, you can build and raise the walls of an addition in a single day.

The difficulties that do arise are not so much in construction as in developing a suitable—and legal—plan for the addition. Zoning regulations place limits on how close you can build to a street or property line, and you may not be able to fit a worthwhile addition within these limits. Nowadays, the builders of most homes make the maximum use permitted of front and side space. As a result an addition built at ground level generally must be placed on the back of the house. Comfort inside the house is another important consideration. Additions commonly have three sides exposed to the elements, where there was only one before. If the addition also happens to be situated on a less sheltered side of the house, the new space can be expensive to heat in winter and to cool in summer.

To save energy, pay special attention to certain construction and design details. Low ceilings and roughly square additions form spaces that can be heated or cooled economically. In a very cold or hot climate, consider altering the conventional 2-by-4 studs shown on pages 46-47 to studs made of 2-by-6s and spaced 24 inches apart; the thicker wall provides room for thicker, more effective insulation. Extra insulation can also be provided by substituting sheets of rigid plastic for plywood as exterior sheathing. Build roof overhangs above the windows on a south wall, to cut the heat of high-angle summer sun but admit low-angle winter sun that helps warm the room. Install double glass or storm sash for each window.

Not every energy-saving idea will work for you. Limiting the number and size of windows in an addition, for example, is tempting but not necessarily desirable. If an addition displaces windows that once admitted light, the house may become too dark. In that situation you may want numerous and large windows in the addition to replace some of the lost light—and you may even decide to install a new window or two in the house itself.

The Bay Window: A Hang-on Addition, Factory-made

A window in a floor-to-ceiling bay is an elegant addition that can convert a small or dark room into a bright alcove for dining, reading or visiting. The one depicted on these and the following pages consists of a cantilevered platform and a knee-height wall built to support a prefabricated window unit that comes from the manufacturer complete with the glass, trim and ceiling. Many window manufacturers also offer easy-to-install prefabricated metal or wooden roofs, which eliminate the complex miter cuts otherwise necessary to frame a roof for a bay window. The model shown below is covered with attractive wooden shakes.

Before deciding on a bay window, find out whether your house is platform framed or balloon framed. Examine your floor joists. If there are no studs alongside them, you have platform framing and can add a bay without hesitation. But if you find studs alongside the floor joists, you have balloon framing. With this type of construction, house ceilings less than 9 feet high will not accommodate the headroom of the bay.

In most cases, no foundation is needed for a bay window; you simply extend the joists from the house basement to make a cantilevered platform by one of the methods shown below. However, if your house is constructed on a slab, you will have to build a slab *(page 41)* for the bay. If your house has only a crawl space, you can still extend the joists, but the work will be cramped and you may prefer to build a foundation for the bay.

Bay-window units are available in heights of 4 to 6 feet, widths of 5 to 9 feet, and depths of 17 to 24 inches; they can be ordered with sides meeting the house at 30° or 45° angles. The height you choose depends in part on the ceiling height in your house and the depth of the header that will be necessary to span the bay opening *(page 28)*.

With few exceptions, installing a bay window involves only basic carpentry and masonry. One exception is the case of a house with a solid-masonry wall; unless you are experienced in heavy masonry work, you may need a professional to open such a wall for the bay. Other exceptions are a bay on a house of post-and-beam construction, or one less than 4 feet from a corner of a house; in both cases special precautions prescribed by a structural engineer are needed to avoid weakening the house structure.

Although a bay window is small compared to most additions, it requires permits in most localities. Order the prefabricated bay window at least two weeks in advance so that it will be on hand when you are ready to begin work.

Two Ways of Extending a Floor

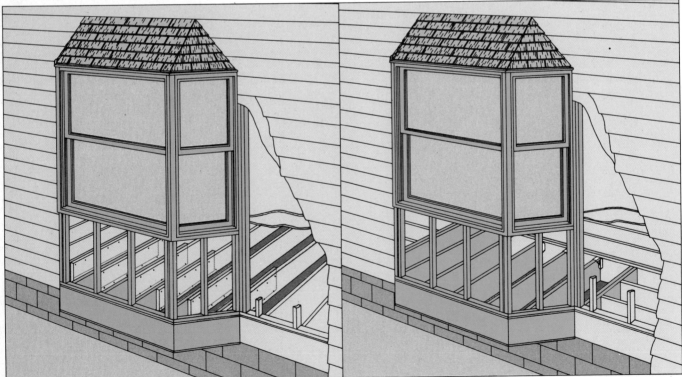

Parallel and perpendicular joists. The platforms for these bay windows differ only in the way they are grafted to the house. In the installation at left, where the floor joists in the house run perpendicular to the exterior wall, bay joists are simple extensions spliced to the floor joists *(page 24)*. Where existing floor joists run parallel to the exterior wall *(right)*, the bay joists run at right angles to the house joists, which are cut away and reinforced *(pages 24-26)*.

22

Getting at the Joists

1 **Laying out the rough opening.** Inside the house, mark the width of the bay-window rough opening on the baseboard. With a plumb bob steadied by a helper, transfer the two marks to the top of the wall. Drill through the wall at all four points to mark the width of the opening on the outside. In platform framing, remove the baseboard and cut away the wallboard from floor to ceiling between the studs that bracket the drilled holes. In balloon framing, remove wallboard an additional stud space beyond the holes. Mark the width of the rough opening on the sole plate of the house or, if you have balloon framing, on the floor.

2 **Removing the siding.** As a guide in cutting the siding, snap vertical chalk lines outside the house from the top of the wall to the bottom, linking the holes that you drilled in Step 1. Snap a horizontal chalk line at the level of the ceiling inside the house, then cut through the siding along the lines with a circular saw set to the thickness of the siding.

Caution: Always wear goggles and a respirator when using a circular saw, and use a saw with a carbide-tipped blade to avoid damaging the saw in case you hit a nail. Within the entire area marked by the cut lines you have made, pry the siding from the wall (*page 35, Step 2*).

3 **Exposing the floor joists.** Transfer the distance between the floor and the lower holes drilled in Step 1 to the sheathing outside. Snap a horizontal chalk line between the two points, then set a circular saw to the thickness of the sheathing and cut along the chalk line. Extend the saw blade and cut the sheathing vertically at the sawed ends of siding.

Pry off enough sheathing to expose the stringer, then reset the saw to cut 1⅝ inches deeper and cut through the joist at both ends of the opening. Have a helper in the basement knock the cut ends of the stringer out with a 4-pound sledge; with the stringer out of the way, you have clear access to the other floor joists.

For a house that has a brick veneer, use a reciprocating saw instead of a circular saw.

23

A Simple Splice of Joists

Splicing the bay joists. If existing floor joists run perpendicular to the wall where the bay will be installed, mark each joist within the rough opening at a point twice the depth of the bay window, measuring from the joist's outer end. Then, from lumber the same size as the existing floor joists, cut joist extensions 6 inches longer than three times the depth of the bay. Slide the extensions through the wall over the sill, hammering if necessary, until their inner ends align with the marks on the floor joists. If your house is balloon framed, avoid studs alongside joists by positioning the extensions on the opposite side of the joists. Nail the extensions to the floor joists with 16-penny nails every 10 inches in a zigzag pattern (*inset*).

If joists run parallel to the wall where the bay will be installed, follow the procedure below.

A New Pattern of Joists

1 Rearranging joists. Mark the width of the rough opening on the floor joist nearest the basement wall and extend the marks across the bottoms of the floor joists with a chalk line to twice the depth of the bay. Mark for removal the joist sections between the wall and that point.

2 Reinforcing a joist. Increase the strength of the next joist beyond those to be cut, by nailing a reinforcement joist to it with 16-penny nails in a zigzag pattern. Then install blocking between the reinforced joist and the next joist beyond it, to keep these joists in alignment.

REINFORCED JOIST

TOP PLATE

TOP PLATE

BOTTOM PLATE

TOP PLATE

BOTTOM PLATE

3 **Supporting the floor.** Install 4-by-4 shoring across the joists between the outside wall and the reinforced joist, locating it 2 feet to either side of the chalk lines made in Step 1. The support posts are toenailed to the top plates—use a plumb line to make sure that the posts will be directly beneath the reinforced joist and the floor joist nearest to the basement wall. These assemblies are raised onto the bottom plates, plumbed and shimmed for a tight fit, then toenailed to the bottom plates.

4 **Cutting the floor joists.** Cut the joists marked for removal 3 inches beyond the rough-opening marks, using a saber saw until it hits the flooring above. Complete the cuts with a handsaw. Pry the severed joists downward (and away from studs if your house is balloon framed) until the flooring nails are visible. Cut the nails with a cold chisel to remove the joist sections.

5 Providing headers. Install headers—doubled joist lumber long enough to reach from the reinforced joist to the cut edge of the stringer—at either side of the rough opening. Butt-nail the headers against the ends of cut joists, then toenail the headers to the stringer and to the reinforced joist. Attach double joist hangers to connect the headers to the reinforced joist, to the cut joists and to the cut stringer.

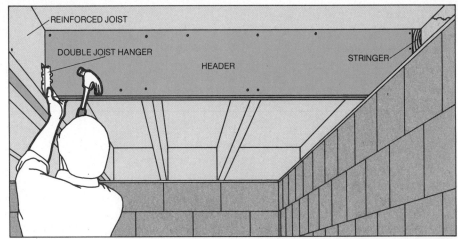

REINFORCED JOIST

DOUBLE JOIST HANGER

HEADER

STRINGER

6 Installing the bay joists. Slide bay joists, cut 6 inches longer than the distance from the reinforced house joist to the outside wall of the bay, through the wall and fasten them to joist hangers nailed upside down to the reinforced joist at 16-inch intervals. Use metal anchors (*inset*) to secure the joists to the sill plate. From above, nail the flooring to the new joists.

Completing the Platform

1 Cutting a platform pattern. Set a strip of ½-inch exterior plywood on top of the window and mark side reference points at the edges of the window casing. Using these reference points, cut out a bay-shaped plywood pattern and cut an identical piece of plywood for later use as subflooring. Set the pattern on top of the bay joists so that it butts against the house subflooring; mark the outline of the pattern on the joists.

CASING

2 Fitting the bay header joists. Set a piece of joist lumber along a side edge of the pattern and mark the length of the side on the board, shifting the plywood on the joists as necessary. Tilt a circular-saw blade to the bay angle and cut the board at the marks. Make a similar piece for the other side, then cut a front header joist with square ends to fit between the side pieces *(inset)*.

3 Trimming the joists. Set a piece of 2-by-4 scrap on edge atop the bay joists, its outside face flush with the marks made in Step 1, opposite. Against the inside face of the 2-by-4, make a second set of marks on the joists, and cut off the joist ends at these marks. Butt-nail the front header-joist section to the bay-joist ends, and toe-nail the side sections to the front section and to the house joist.

Nail the plywood pattern to the undersides of the bay joists, fill the spaces between joists with loose-fill or blanket insulation, and nail the sub-flooring that you cut in Step 1 *(opposite)* to the top edges of the bay joists.

Framing and Fitting the Window

The wide opening you must cut through a wall to accommodate a walk-in bay window is framed like the opening for a doorway—studs at the sides position a header that spans the opening.

Headers consist of ½-inch plywood or steel sandwiched between two pieces of 2-inch structural-grade lumber. Steel permits the use of narrower lumber—providing a shallower header that gives more headroom. Order the plate predrilled with the number of boltholes per foot required by code.

The width of the lumber, and thus the depth of the header, depend on the materials used, the distance spanned and whether the opening is in a bearing wall or a nonbearing one (chart below). Bearing walls run at right angles to joists; nonbearing ones run parallel to them.

If you are installing the header in a bearing wall, shore the ceiling joists of a platform-framed house (page 22), the most common type, as described here. For a balloon-framed house, follow the method overleaf. For an opening in a second-floor bearing wall, erect shoring on the ground floor and second floor.

Header Sizes for Wall Openings

Opening location	Span of opening (in feet)				
	4	6	8	10	12
Roof only or nonbearing wall in one- or two-story house	2 × 4	2 × 6	2 × 8	2 × 10	2 × 12
Bearing wall in one-story house or on second floor of two-story house	2 × 6	2 × 8	2 × 10	2 × 12	—
Bearing wall on first floor of two-story house	2 × 10	2 × 10	2 × 12	—	—

Choosing a header. The chart at left lists lumber widths required for plywood-reinforced headers for openings in nonbearing and bearing walls in one- and two-story houses. Use the section of the chart that describes the opening you plan, then look up the span required. Use structural-grade lumber and, if the span lies between the widths listed in the chart, use the header for the next larger opening. If there is no entry on the chart for your opening and span, or if you have a roof-mounted air conditioner or live in an area of heavy snowfalls or high winds, use a steel-reinforced header. Consult a structural engineer about the correct size of such a header.

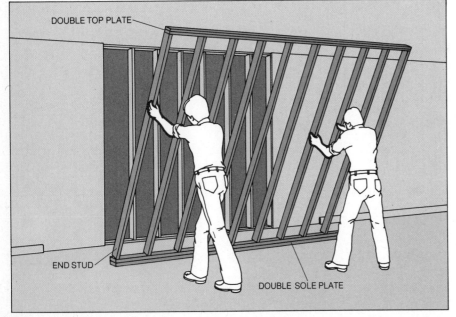

DOUBLE TOP PLATE

END STUD

DOUBLE SOLE PLATE

A Rough Opening in a Platform-framed Wall

1 Shoring the ceiling. For an opening in a nonbearing wall, no ceiling support is needed; simply use a 4-pound sledge to knock out the wall studs in the rough opening. For an opening in a bearing wall, erect a temporary partition between floor and ceiling. Nail to the floor, 4 feet from the wall, a doubled 2-by-4 sole plate 4 feet longer than the width of the rough opening. Set a single 2-by-4 top plate next to the doubled plate and mark both plates for studs on 16-inch centers. Cut studs 6¼ inches shorter than the distance from floor to ceiling, butt-nail them to the top plate, then double the top plate.

With a helper, lift the assembly onto the sole plate, plumb the end studs and toenail them to the bottom plate. Plumb and toenail the other studs and shim the partition tight against the ceiling. Brace the partition with a diagonal 1-by-4. Remove the studs in the rough opening.

2 **Installing king and jack studs.** At the rough-opening mark located on the sole plate at each side of the opening *(page 23, Step 1)*, lay out positions for jack studs and a king stud. Toenail a king stud between the sole plate and the top plate. Nail to the opening side of each king stud and to the sole plate a doubled jack stud long enough to reach the bottom of the header.

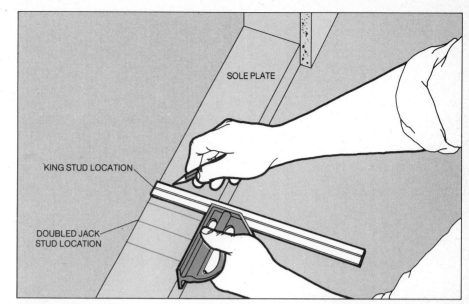

3 **Nailing the header.** Cut two lengths of header lumber *(chart, opposite)* to fit between the king studs. If you are using ½-inch plywood reinforcement, cut it to fit between the header boards, assemble the three pieces, and fasten them together from both sides with 16-penny nails driven every 10 inches in a staggered pattern.

If you are using a steel reinforcement plate, use it as a template to drill boltholes in the boards, then bolt the pieces together.

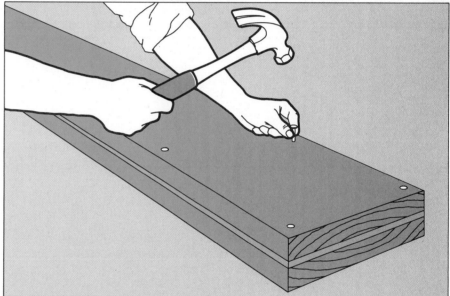

4 **Installing a header.** With a helper, set the completed header on top of the jack studs. On each side of the opening, drive six 16-penny nails through the side of the king stud into the end of the header. (For clarity, the shoring has been omitted in this drawing.)

An Opening in a Balloon-framed Wall

1 **Supporting the studs.** While your helpers hold a heavy brace called a whaler—a 2-by-8 board that you have cut about 4 feet longer than the width of the planned bay-window opening—against the studs and the ceiling, nail the whaler to the studs at each side of the opening in the wall. Then secure the whaler firmly to each stud within the opening with a ⅜-inch lag bolt placed about 2 inches above the bottom of the whaler. Nail short 2-by-8 planks flat to the floor directly beneath the ends of the whaler.

Cut two 4-by-4 posts to fit between the whaler and the planks and install a post at each end of the whaler. Shim the posts tightly against the whaler and toenail them to both the whaler and the plank. Then build a temporary bearing partition, following the method shown on page 28, Step 1. Remove the studs and firestops inside the window opening, sawing them off flush with the whaler unless your ceilings are very high. In that case a prebuilt bay window may not fit properly unless you cut the studs lower to provide for a greater drop in the ceiling of the bay.

2 **Installing the header.** Cut two 2-by-4s long enough to reach from the sill plate—or from the top of a floor joist if one is in the way—to a height you have chosen for the bottom of the header. Face-nail these as jack studs to wall studs at the sides of the window opening, then toenail the jack studs to the sill plate or joist. Build a header (*page 29, Step 3*) and install it on top of the jack studs (*inset*).

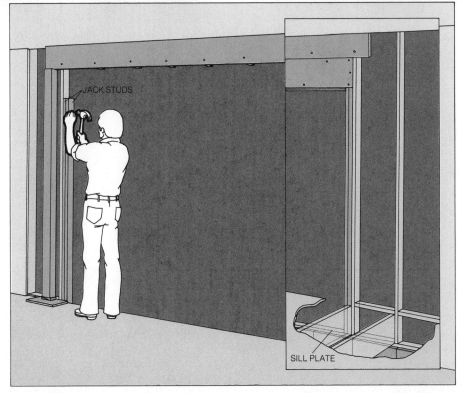

JACK STUDS

SILL PLATE

3 **Completing the rough opening.** Mark the floor for two studs at each side of the rough opening. Cut four studs and nail them together in pairs. Align the doubled studs with the floor marks and toenail the tops to the window header. Toenail the bottoms to the doubled header in the basement *(page 26, Step 5)* or, if you are splicing joists, to the sill plate atop the foundation. Remove the whaler and temporary shoring.

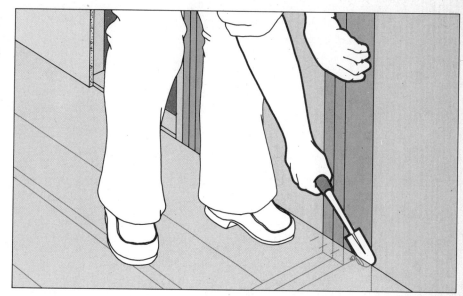

Building the Knee Wall

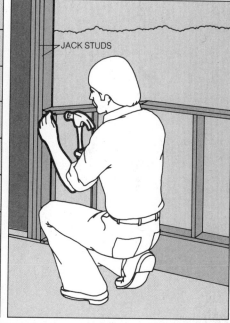

JACK STUDS

1 **Assembling the knee wall.** After removing sheathing—and the sole plate, in a platform-framed house—within the rough opening, make three knee-wall sections to support the window. Mark and cut top plates and sole plates the same way as joist pieces *(page 27, Step 2)*, then cut studs 3½ inches shorter than the difference between header height and bay-window height. For the middle wall, butt-nail plates to studs, putting end studs at the ends of the plates. For the side walls, trim the house ends of the plates as shown in the inset, then position end studs so that they bear fully on the plates.

2 **Installing the walls.** Set one side wall at the edge of the platform. Use tenpenny nails to secure the ends of the top and sole plates to the jack studs and the sole plate to the joist that outlines the bay platform. Also, nail the end stud to the jack studs. Install the other side wall the same way, then set the center wall between the side walls. Nail the end studs of the center wall to the end studs of the side walls, then nail the sole plate to the joist.

Sheathe the knee wall *(page 48)*. If the window you are using is built to butt against house sheathing, cut away a 1½-inch strip of siding, from knee wall to header. If the window is to fit against siding, leave the siding uncut.

Installing the Window

1 **Positioning the window.** Remove the seat-board brace from the window, and with one helper for every 3 feet of window width, tilt the unit and lift it onto the knee wall. Butt the brickmold against the exposed sheathing or, for some window units, against the siding. Center the window between the jack studs and brace it in the opening with two 2-by-4s tacked to the window mullions and to stakes in the ground.

2 **Leveling the window unit.** To determine where to place shims for leveling, use a level to find the high side of the front window, then nail the window frame at that side of the unit to the top plate of the front knee wall 2 inches inside the corner of the window. At the low side, shim between the knee-wall top plate and the window frame until the frame is level, using slate instead of wooden shims for windows that are 8 feet wide or more. Nail the window to the knee wall every 6 inches, nailing through the shims if they are wooden.

3 **Plumbing the window.** Cut 2-by-4 nailing blocks to fit between the header and the top of the knee wall; nail the blocks to the jack studs at the edges of the rough opening. Plane a bevel on the edge of each piece to match the angle of the bay and leave a clearance of ½ inch between the bevel and the window-end jamb when the block is nailed to the jack stud *(inset).* Plumb by driving wooden shims between the blocks and the end jamb, then secure the shims with tenpenny finishing nails.

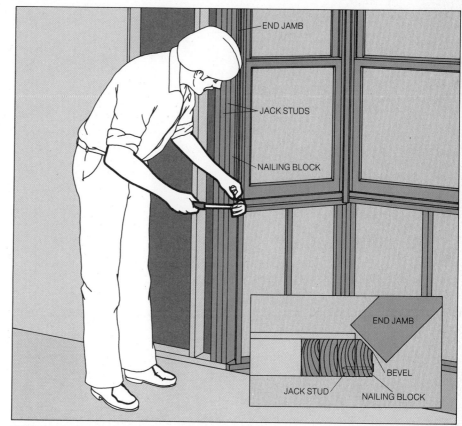

4 **Securing the headboard.** Wedge the window in place by pounding wooden shims every 8 inches between the headboard and the header. Nail through the headboard and the shims and into the header; fill gaps with insulation.

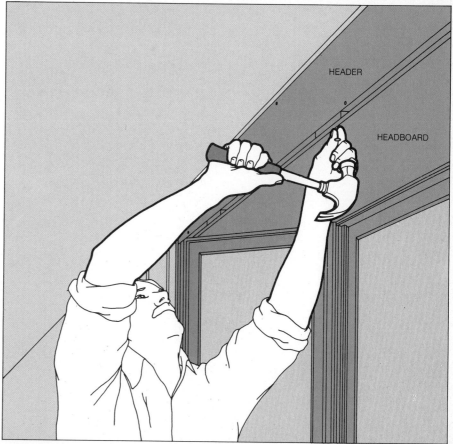

Adding a Precut Roof

1 **Marking the siding.** After nailing the precut drip cap to the top of the window, have a helper assist in positioning the center section of precut roof sheathing between the drip cap and the wall. Then, while your helper holds the triangular side pieces of sheathing in place, outline the sheathing on the siding. Cut along the lines with a circular saw set to a depth of ¾ inch; saw as far as you can, then complete the diagonal cuts near the top of the window with a chisel.

DRIP CAP

2 **Removing the siding.** Working from top to bottom within the saw cuts, pry the siding off. About 10 inches above the headboard and directly opposite the mullion at each end of the center window, fasten a length of perforated metal strap to the bay header behind the sheathing, using ½-inch lag bolts and washers. Pull each strap taut and bolt it to a mullion. Cover the headboard with insulation.

MULLION

HEADBOARD

3 **Installing rafters.** Between the drip cap and the top of the opening in the siding, toenail the precut hip rafters that come with the roof, placing them between the mullions and the top corners of the area of exposed sheathing. Next, attach end rafters flat against the house wall, nailing them to the drip cap, the hip rafters and the sheathing. Then nail the remaining rafters to the headboard and sheathing, spacing them equally between the hip rafters. Nail the roof sheathing to the rafters.

With galvanized roof nails, nail the preformed metal drip edge that comes with the window to the lower edge of the roof sheathing. Then flash the roof (*pages 64-65*) and cover it according to the manufacturer's instructions for the roofing material you choose.

HIP RAFTER

HEADER

Foundations to Support an Added Room

An addition that looks like a part of the original house plan rather than an after-thought begins with a foundation that is not only structurally sound but allows you to match the floor level in the house and to make a seamless extension of a house wall, if you wish.

The problem of matching the floor levels is generally attacked by building the foundation of the addition flush with the top of the house foundation. You can compensate for slight differences in lumber dimensions or errors in building the foundation by shimming or notching floor framing members—or sleepers, in the case of a slab—to make the addition subflooring flush with that of the house.

If the addition will extend an interior wall of the house, you must place the foundation so that you can tie the addition wall to the end framing of the house wall. And where you are extending the façade of your house, the addition foundation generally should line up with the house foundation.

In a frame house finished with shingles, clapboards or metal siding, you can find the subfloor level, the top or side of the foundation, and the end framing of

walls simply by removing a strip of siding and sheathing from the bottom of the wall as shown below, a step also necessary to install joists for the addition floor. You may also have to chip away some of the waterproofing mortar on many block foundations to place the addition building line flush with the house foundation.

Brick-veneer, solid-brick or block construction complicates the task of positioning the foundation. To mark the floor level or the end of an interior wall, for example, you must measure carefully inside the house from a door, a window or a pilot hole, then transfer the distances outside. The top of the new foundation is found by measuring down from floor level a distance equal to the total height of new-floor framing members. To find the foundation side of a brick-veneer house, you may have to dig below the brick.

What kind of foundation to build for the addition depends on the house foundation. If your house has a basement or crawl space, for example, build a crawl-space foundation for your addition as detailed on these and the following pages. If joists of your addition will span more than 15 feet, add piers for a girder (page

114). If your house rests on a slab, choose between two concrete-slab foundations (page 41). If the house slab rises no more than 12 inches above ground and if the footings of the new slab need to descend no deeper than 2 feet below grade to reach below the frost line, a turned-down slab is adequate. But if the slab must be built higher than 12 inches, or if unstable soil makes it difficult to dig the narrow trenches necessary to form the turned-down edge of the slab, build a combination slab-on-block foundation.

If the ground drops more than 24 inches from the house to the outer wall of the proposed addition, a crawl-space foundation will be the most economical choice, regardless of your house foundation. But if the land drops as much as 36 inches, you may need a stepped foundation, a complicated structure that requires considerable expertise to build.

After excavating a foundation that conforms to the local code, have the trenches checked by the building inspector. If your soil is wet or poorly compacted, more digging may be necessary to reach firm soil, or you may require a professionally designed, stronger foundation.

A Three-Sided Foundation

1 Attaching the marker boards. After removing a strip of siding and sheathing (page 23) about 15 inches high—or extending to at least 1 inch above the sole plate—between the corners of the addition, nail two 8-foot 1-by-4 marker boards, shimmed to make up for missing siding, flush with the top of the house foundation. The boards should extend 3½ feet inside the corners marked at the house. Center a nail in the top edge of each marker board at the corners.

If the addition will extend an interior house wall, position the nail 4 inches—8 inches if you are going to finish the addition with brick veneer—outside the inner edge of the tie-in stud. If you are extending an exterior wall, align the corner nail with the house foundation.

TIE-IN STUD

MARKER BOARD

2 Making the addition square. Lay out building lines using the 3-4-5 triangle method. To do this, drive a nail at the center of the marker-board edge, 3 feet from a corner nail. Have two helpers cross measuring tapes hooked to the two nails so that the 4-foot mark on the corner-nail tape meets the 5-foot mark on the other tape. Drive a 3-foot stake at this point, then drive a nail into the top of the stake. Position a similar stake opposite the other marker board.

Use string to extend the line between the corner nails in the marker boards and the nails in the stakes. Drive stakes to mark the ends of the addition side walls. Measure the diagonals of the resulting rectangle; if they are not equal, move the end stakes to make them so.

3 Building and marking batter boards. With a water level, mark the height of the house foundation on 2-by-4s driven to form right angles at the end stakes, 5 feet beyond the building lines. Then nail 1-by-6 batter boards, aligning the top edges with the marks. Stretch strings from the marker boards to extend the building lines to the batter boards. Drive nails in the boards to mark the lines. Drive nails into the batter boards and marker boards for the foundation wall and the footing trench and main trench, using the dimensions shown in the inset. (For brick veneer, drive the foundation-wall nails 11⅝ inches inside the building lines.) Remove the end stakes and dig the trenches so that the top of the footing trench lies a multiple of 8 inches below the top of the house foundation.

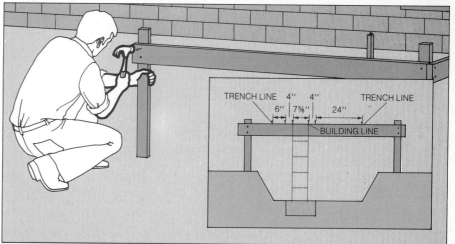

4 Leveling the trench. After driving 1-by-2 stakes at the corners of the footing trench—and every 3 feet along it in a zigzag pattern, 3 inches from the sides—mark the top of the footing trench on one stake and transfer the mark to the other stakes with a water level. Deepen the footing trench where marks are less than 8 inches from the bottom; do not fill in the trench where it is deeper than 8 inches.

Drive two 16-inch lengths of ½-inch reinforcing bar, called grade pegs, on each side of the trench adjacent to each corner stake, and level with the mark. Remove the corner stakes and tamp the dirt around each grade peg.

5 **Pouring the footing.** Place two lengths of No. 4 reinforcing bar on bricks in the footing trench and wire the bars to the grade pegs. Where two pieces of bar meet, overlap them 16 inches and wire them together. Pour the footing so that the concrete comes to the tops of the grade pegs, and let the concrete cure under sheets of polyethylene for 24 hours.

Run taut strings between the building-line nails on the batter boards and marker boards; then transfer the lines to the footing with a plumb bob and chalk line. Now you can remove the strings, batter boards and marker boards.

6 **Beginning the foundation wall.** Lay a dry run for the first course of the foundation, then lay stepped sets of blocks three courses high as leads at the corners and ends of the foundation. Lay the block walls using a mason's line as a guide. Place wire-mesh reinforcement into the mortar bed of every third course of blocks.

On opposite sides of the addition, install two ventilators in place of foundation blocks in the middle of the wall. Pack mortar around the edges, sloping the bottom for drainage. In the next course, lay solid blocks over each vent.

If you intend to finish the addition with brick veneer, build the wall with 12-inch blocks to a point immediately below ground level, and complete the wall with 8-inch blocks laid flush with the inside of the foundation wall.

7 Setting anchor bolts. Lay mesh reinforcement under the top course of the foundation, fill the cores of the top course with mortar and, before the mortar sets, install anchor bolts for the sill plate 1 foot from each corner and doorway and every 4 feet in between. Use ½-inch anchor bolts 8 inches long and position each with a piece of 2-by-6 that has a ⅝-inch hole drilled in the center. Insert the bolt in the hole, fit a washer and nut, then set the 2-by-6 back ½ inch from the outside of the foundation wall or, if you are extending an exterior wall, match the setback of the house sill plate. Tap the anchor bolt into the mortar as far as it will go. After 24 hours, remove the nuts and washers and lift the 2-by-6 jigs from the bolts.

8 Installing the sill plate. Place atop the wall a pressure-treated 2-by-6 that is ½ inch shorter than a foundation side wall (measured from the house sill plate), and use a combination square to mark it with the anchor-bolt locations. Drill ¾-inch holes centered at the marks.

Install a layer of sill sealer, available in rolls 6 inches wide, and bolt the sill plate on. Install the remaining sill plates in the same fashion, shim them level and check them for squareness, then toenail the ends together.

Tying the New Floor to the Old

1 Installing header and stringer joists. Cut a header joist equal to the distance between the outside edges of the side-wall sill plates and fasten it to the exposed joist on the house, using ½-inch lag bolts 4 inches long and 16 inches apart in a zigzag pattern, starting 2 inches from one end of the joist. Do not bolt a joist to brick veneer; toenail it to the sill plates at each end.

Toenail two stringer joists 3 inches shorter than the side-wall sill plates to the header joist. Butt-nail another header joist to the stringer joists and toenail all three to the sill plates.

2 Securing floor joists and subfloor. Install joists the same size as those on the house every 16 inches, butt-nailing them to the sill joists where possible or using joist hangers or anchors. Toenail blocking between joists every 4 feet.

After filling the trenches inside the walls, cover the earth within a crawl space with 6-mil polyethylene sheeting weighted down with rocks as a vapor barrier. Staple insulation between the joists then install subflooring, leaving an area in the center of the floor temporarily uninsulated and uncovered for access to the crawl space for utility work. Waterproof the outside of the foundation with a ½-inch layer of mortar up to grade level —or higher, to match your house.

Trowel asphalt waterproofing onto the mortar below grade, then fill the trench outside the walls. For drainage, slope the earth outside at least ¼ inch per foot to a distance of 6 feet.

Precision Fitting for a Concrete Slab

A slab foundation. Most slabs rest on a block wall and footings identical to those built for a crawl-space foundation *(Steps 1-6, pages 36-38)*, except that air vents are omitted and the final course of the wall is laid with L-shaped header blocks to form a shelf. The area between the foundation walls is filled with compacted gravel to the level of the slab shelf, the gravel is cov-

ered with 6-mil polyethylene, and expansion-joint material is placed along the house.

The other three sides of the slab, and part of the bottom, are insulated with rigid styrofoam insulation. Wire mesh reinforces the slab. Sole plates are attached with anchor bolts set into mortar-filled cores of the blocks. In warm climates

the block foundation shown here can be omitted. Instead, use simple forms and footing trenches to shape the concrete poured for the slab into turned-down edges that will serve as both footing and foundation. Reinforcing bars strengthen the edge of the foundation, mesh strengthens the slab itself. Anchor bolts for sole plates are set into the wet concrete.

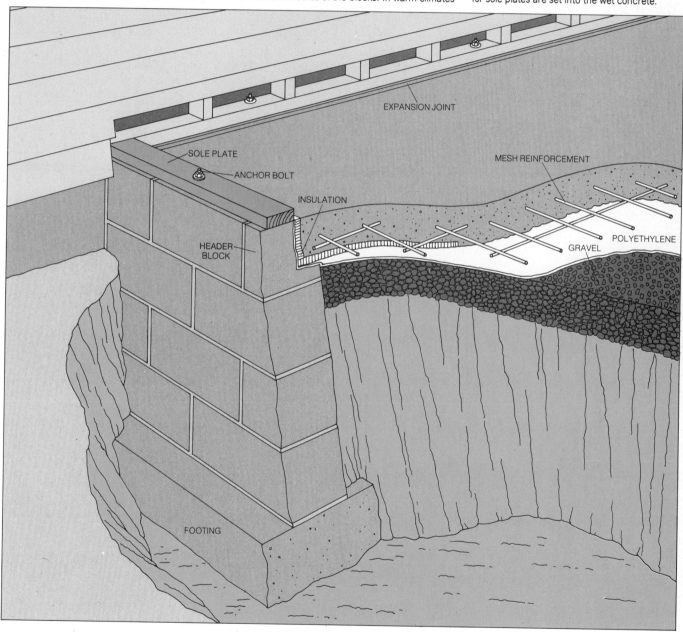

EXPANSION JOINT

SOLE PLATE

ANCHOR BOLT

MESH REINFORCEMENT

INSULATION

POLYETHYLENE

HEADER BLOCK

GRAVEL

FOOTING

Grafting New Walls to the Side of a House

Erecting the walls, the most impressive stage in the construction of an addition, is also the simplest. In a single day, stud walls—made from vertical 2-by-4s and horizontal top and sole plates—can be assembled, tilted upright, tied to the house, braced, and covered with sheathing. The process differs from standard wall construction only at the joint between the house and the addition wall.

To tie the addition to a house that has wooden siding or stucco, you have to cut through the siding and sheathing and nail the addition wall to a corner post or to

extra studs that you insert into the house wall. If the existing wall surface is masonry, you bolt the new walls on.

When buying materials, be sure you get perfectly straight 2-by-4s for wall plates and corner and window studs. You can straighten a crooked stud after the walls are upright by making a shallow horizontal saw cut across the inner edge of the stud, pushing the stud straight and nailing a short strip of plywood to each side of it, over the saw cut.

The wall studs for the addition must be the same length as those in the house if

the ceilings are to match. To determine the correct length, make a small hole through the ceiling covering of the existing room next to the addition and measure vertically from a ceiling joist to the finish floor; subtract the distance between the finish floor and the bottom of the studs (measured in Step 1, page 40) and then subtract 3 inches for the double top plate of the new walls.

Make the addition walls plumb, regardless of tilt in the existing walls—to compensate for tilt, angle end studs and adjust the lengths of top plates.

Making the Incisions

1 Marking the siding. If an addition wall will meet the middle of an existing wall, snap a vertical chalk line on the siding ⅝ inch outside the edge of the platform side, then snap another vertical line over the platform, about 12 inches from the first. If the new wall will meet a corner of the existing house, snap a single vertical line about 10 inches from the corner.

Cut the siding along each chalk line as described in Step 2, page 23, then pry away the wall covering between the cuts.

2 Removing the cornice. If the roof overhang extends below the planned height of the addition walls, remove the section of roofing material over the addition platform to expose the roof sheathing. With a framing square, extend the outer two lines you marked in Step 1 onto the frieze board, the soffit, the fascia board and the roof sheathing. Cut the frieze board along both lines with a rented demolition saw—a powerful reciprocating saw with a long straight blade—and pry away the section between the cuts. Cut the soffit and the fascia board along the lines and pry them away. If lookouts supported the soffit (*page 57, bottom*), pry them off.

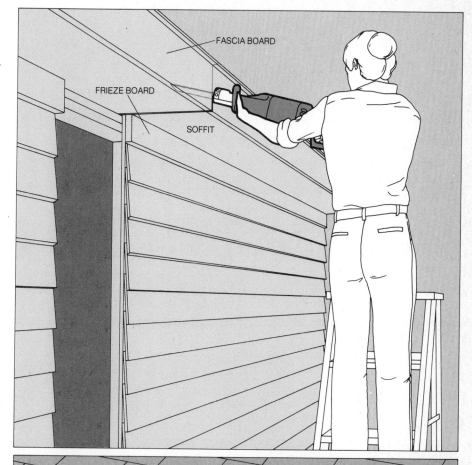

FASCIA BOARD

FRIEZE BOARD

SOFFIT

3 Cutting off the overhang. Drill a pilot hole through the roof sheathing from underneath, directly above each point where the outer face of an addition wall will meet the outer edge of the house-wall top plate. Snap a chalk line between the holes, perpendicular to the two lines you extended across the roof sheathing in Step 2. Cut the roof sheathing along the lines with a circular saw and pry it away from the rafters. With a level, mark a vertical line across each exposed rafter, flush with the outer edge of the top plate; cut the rafters off with a demolition saw.

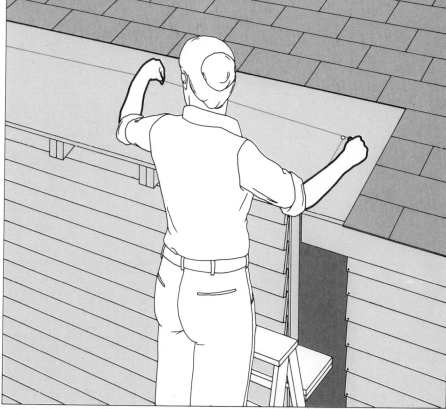

Building Braces into the Cuts

Extra studs for a platform-frame wall. If a new wall will meet the middle of a platform-frame wall, slide a straight stud into the house wall through the slot in the siding and toenail it to top and sole plates flush with the siding. Outside, nail the siding to the stud every 6 inches.

Toenail a second straight stud alongside the first but with its face set flush with the outside edge of the house plates. Slide a third stud alongside the second but perpendicular to it, toenail it to the house plates and then face-nail it to the second stud. If a stud in the house wall blocks the new studs, do not attempt to move it—simply nail the new studs alongside the old one.

Support in a balloon-frame wall. If an addition wall will meet the middle of a balloon-frame wall, remove the interior wall covering opposite the addition wall and nail 2-by-4s horizontally between studs every 2 feet, 1½ inches from the outside edge of the studs. Nail a 2-by-8 vertically where the addition wall will meet the house wall and nail the siding to the 2-by-8.

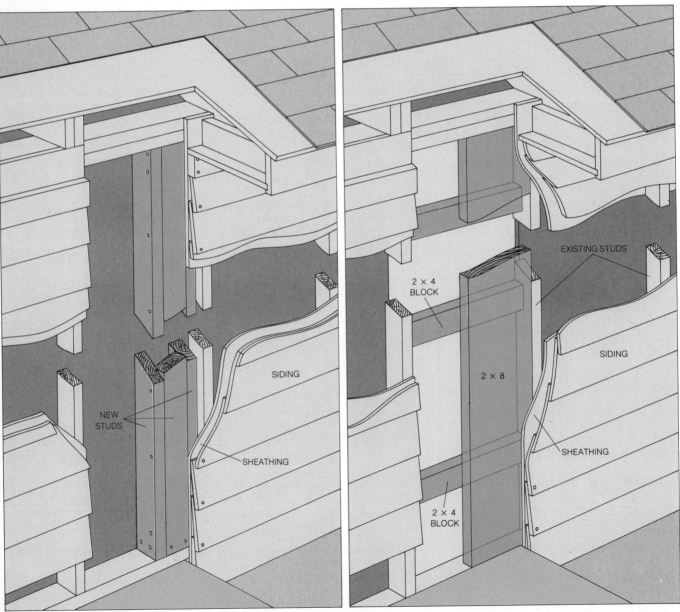

NEW STUDS

SIDING

SHEATHING

2 × 4 BLOCK

EXISTING STUDS

2 × 8

SIDING

SHEATHING

2 × 4 BLOCK

Tying walls to a masonry house. Lay a 2-by-4 flat on the platform as a spacer, hold a stud vertically on the block and flat against the masonry wall, and mark the height of every sixth mortar joint on the edge of the stud. Drill staggered ¼-inch holes through the face of the stud at the marks. Hold the stud against the masonry in exactly the position the new wall will occupy, flush with the outer edge of the platform and on top of the spacer block; plumb the stud with a carpenter's level (*page 47, Step 4*) and fasten it temporarily with masonry nails. Use the stud as a template to drill matching pilot holes in the mortar joints, then remove it. Insert a masonry anchor in each hole. Prepare a stud for the other edge of the platform in the same way.

When you put the addition walls together (*page 46, Step 2*), install the drilled studs at the house end of each side wall; when the walls have been erected, fasten the studs to the house with bolts and washers (*page 47, Step 4*).

SPACER

Assembling the Walls

1 Laying out the plates. If your addition has wooden floor joists, measure from the sole plate of the house (*exposed on page 36, Step 1*) to the edge of the platform end and cut straight 2-by-4 top and sole plates to this length for each side wall; if your addition has a concrete slab foundation, unbolt the sole plates you installed when the slab was poured (*page 41*) and cut top plates to match.

Set the top and sole plates side by side along their respective walls and, measuring from the ends next to the house, mark locations for studs, windows and doors. Determine the width of door and window rough openings from manufacturers' specifications, and mark for jack and king studs beside each. Make end-wall plates 7 inches shorter than the end of the platform; mark them for studs and openings, including an extra nailer stud flush with the ends of the plates if a stud would not fall there normally.

2 **Nailing walls together.** Butt-nail studs to the top and bottom plates at layout marks, omitting the studs for each door or window. For each wall corner, make a post from straight studs and 2-by-4 blocks (*inset*) and nail it to the outer ends of the plates at the corners of the addition.

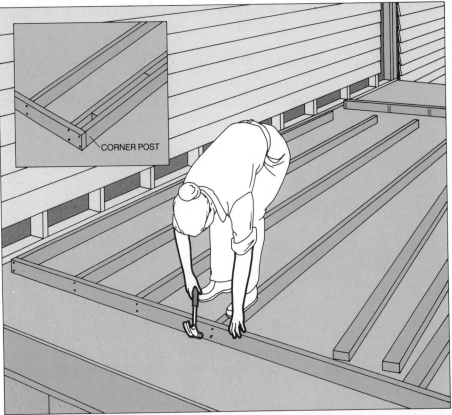

CORNER POST

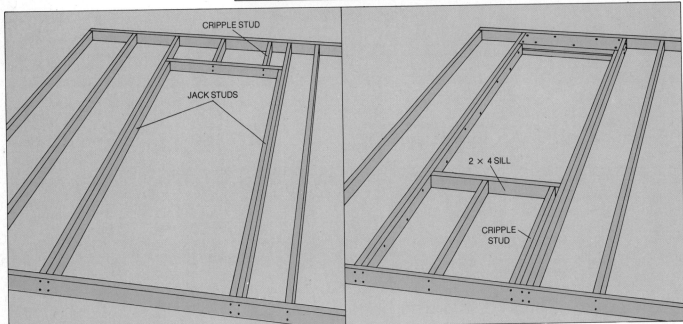

CRIPPLE STUD

JACK STUDS

2 × 4 SILL

CRIPPLE STUD

3 **Framing the rough openings.** Cut jack studs long enough to reach the top of each door rough opening (shown above, left for a nonbearing wall) and nail each to a straight, wall-height stud—called a king stud in this situation—then nail these double studs to the plates to frame each door and window opening. In a bearing wall, make a header for the opening (*chart, page 28*) and nail it horizontally

between the king studs (*page 29, Step 4*). Nail cripple studs, if needed, snugly between the header and the top plate at 16-inch intervals. For a window frame (*above, right*), nail a 2-by-4 sill across the opening and nail cripple studs beneath the sill.

Tilt the wall upright and, if you are building on a slab foundation, slide the predrilled holes in

the sole plate over the anchor bolts, then nail 2-by-4 braces to studs and to the platform every 8 feet along the wall. Drive the end of the sole plate tight against the sole plate of the house wall and flush with the edge of the platform. For a block foundation, nail the sole plate to the stringer or header joist with staggered 16-penny nails at 8-inch intervals; on a slab foundation, bolt the plates down.

4 **Tying the wall to the house.** While a helper holds a 4-foot level against the side of the end stud of the addition wall, push the stud in or out until it is plumb. If you are working in a house made of wood, drive staggered 16-penny nails through the top of the stud into the stud behind it—either the stud you inserted or an existing corner stud of the house; in a masonry house, fasten the stud to masonry anchors, using bolts and washers. In a platform-frame house, toenail the top and sole plates of the addition wall to those of the house wall.

Repeat Steps 1 through 3 to build the other side wall of the addition, then the end wall. Plumb and brace the corner posts of the two side walls first, then the end studs of the end wall.

5 **Straightening the walls.** To eliminate bows in the top plate, stretch a string taut across the surfaces of 2-by-4 blocks at each end of one of the addition walls. Have a helper free the bottom of each brace along the wall; hold a 2-by-4 block between the string and the top plate and push or pull the wall until the string barely touches the 2-by-4, then have your helper renail the brace. Adjust the other walls similarly.

When all of the walls are straight, nail the studs at each end of the end wall to the corner posts of the side walls. Lap a second top plate for the end wall, 7 inches longer than the first one, over the original top plates of the side walls and nail it to the original plates; then nail a second top plate to each of the side walls.

2 × 4 BLOCK

HEADER

2 × 4 BLOCK

6 Sheathing the walls. Have a helper hold a sheet of ½-inch plywood horizontally against the studs; the bottom of the plywood should be flush with the bottom of the sill plate and one end should be tight against the house-wall sole plate. Fasten the plywood to the sill plate, the header or stringer joist and the studs with six-penny nails every 6 inches around the edges and every 12 inches in the center of the sheet. Continue the sheathing horizontally around the addition; when you come to a window or door-way, nail the sheathing in place, snap chalk lines along the edges of the opening and cut the sheathing with a circular saw.

Start the second course with a piece of ply-wood 4 feet square, so that the joints between the sheets are staggered with those in the first course. For the third course, cut the sheets to the width required before you nail them up.

A Glassed-in Sunroom

In this energy-conscious age, builders rarely include a glassed-in Florida sun-room in new houses—even in Florida. They could be making a mistake, for a sunroom can be surprisingly energy-efficient. In cool weather, sunlight can warm a glassed-in room to summer temperatures during the day; at night, insulation and a snugly fitting door in the house wall will keep heat from leak-ing away from the house. In summer, ventilation through sunroom windows often can substitute for air condition-ing—and when air conditioning is nec-essary, the addition can be closed off.

A sunroom—for relaxation or for use as a greenhouse-like plant room—is an addition easy to build but it requires professional assistance in design. Be-cause the walls contain so many win-dows, they are relatively weak; the size of headers and the size and spacing of studs should be specified by an archi-tect or structural engineer.

A sunroom generally is fitted with a concrete-slab floor (page 41), awning and jalousie windows and a shed roof

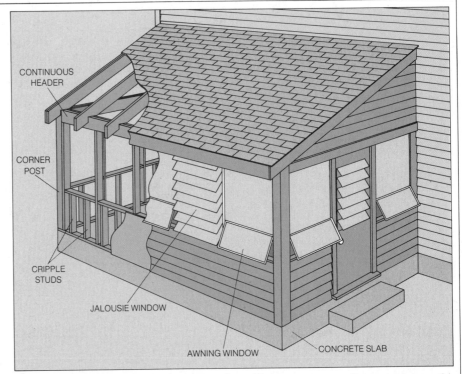

CONTINUOUS HEADER

CORNER POST

CRIPPLE STUDS

JALOUSIE WINDOW

AWNING WINDOW

CONCRETE SLAB

(pages 58-59). The walls of the typical sunroom, shown above, resemble the stud walls shown on the preceding pages, with one important difference: a continuous header runs the length of each sunroom wall, combining the functions of separate rough-framing headers and conventional 2-by-4 top plates. The header ends are supported by jack studs nailed to heavy posts.

A Home that Grows Up with the Family

Many a visitor to a remodeled old house has admired the spacious kitchen—only to be told by the proud owner, "Oh, this was originally the entire house. Everything else was added on later."

Adding on is an American tradition. The practice began with the first settlers at Plymouth Rock—it gave rise to a uniquely American style of architecture, the rambling New England farmhouse *(below)*—and it continues unabated today as homeowners expand to provide for growing families, to add amenities to a simple structure, and to relieve the monotony of look-alike tract houses.

The farmhouse grew, first in New England, later in the Midwest, from a single room and fireplace. A parlor was added to the other side of the chimney; then, in no particular order, came a shed-roofed lean-to, a dormer, a proper second story, and entire wings that swallowed up the original cottage. The result has become an American symbol of home.

If style was the accidental result of traditional farmhouse expansion, it was the goal in many additions. When Thomas Jefferson moved in 1801 into the White House, which was then an uninspired copy of an English manor house, he thought it lacked dignity. With the great architect Benjamin Latrobe, he designed additions—imposing porticoes to the north and south, low terrace-pavilions to the east and west—that helped to create today's quiet grandeur.

On a lesser scale, both style and necessity have spurred modern adding-on. Homes now are mass-produced by the hundreds, with nearly identical designs placed side by side on nearly identical lots. During the early years of marriage many young families happily settle for four rooms of their own. Upgrading such cramped quarters into roomy, distinctive residences is a challenge. How well it has been met across the United States is demonstrated by the examples on the following pages, all of them small development houses that their owners have transformed by adding on.

An American rambler. Extending in several directions, this Maine home has the informal charm that makes the New England farmhouse an American classic.

Upgrading a
Cookie-Cutter House

"Instant slum" was one of the kinder characterizations of Levittown, the community of 17,000 houses that in five years sprang up on a potato farm in a New York City suburb. Although houses differed in such details as paint color, there were only two basic models; the later version is the one illustrated here.

The doomsayers were wrong. Additions have made nearly every house individual. No longer need a Levittowner, arriving home, pause to be sure he has the right house.

Two wings for doubled space. Adding rearward wings that nestle the patio in a U kept the owner—an architect—busy for 2½ years. The wings contain a master bedroom and bath *(left)* and a living room and play loft *(right)*.

The original. This 1951 Levittown house, one of the few still unmodified a generation later, shows how the houses at bottom and right originally looked. It has four rooms and it cost $7,990 new—a TV set and the fireplace included.

A dormer studio. A comparatively small dormer built onto the rear gave the owner, a graphic designer, a home studio. He bought the house new in 1951, intending from the beginning to incorporate additions. The dormer was the first.

A real picture window. Because almost the entire outer wall of the dormer is window, the garden view is part of the room and the small, low-ceilinged studio seems larger than it really is.

Expanding a Ranch House

The homes below and opposite, two next-door neighbors in an Atlanta subdivision, indicate the dramatic impact additions can have. Both began as identical five-room ranch houses. One became strikingly modern, nestled into its hillside, while the other acquired touches of the colonial style in an extensive expansion and remodeling, with the original rooms replanned to accommodate large outdoor parties.

These two houses are part of a development of several hundred. Although there were six models and a variety of roofing and siding materials, all were built in a one-story ranch style with a porch. Over the years their owners, reluctant to leave an enjoyable neighborhood, built additions that make them different.

The original. The basic Atlanta house has two bedrooms, bath, kitchen, living room and dining room on one floor of 1,500 square feet. The buyer could specify the location of the porch and choose siding and roofing materials.

Making the most of a hillside. In an addition that replaces the original porch, the rear wall is set into a hill in the backyard. The new wing contains an entire suite of rooms—a den and a master bedroom with bath.

Remaking the house. The complex additions above changed virtually every room in the house. The rear of the house was extended to make a new dining room behind the French doors at left and expand the old dining room (behind the doors at right) into a family room. A bay window provided a breakfast nook for the kitchen. A master-bedroom wing was added at right.

A light and airy alcove. Within the wallpapered nook formed by the bay window, a wrought-iron breakfast table and chairs look out toward the sunny patio and the master-bedroom wing.

Bold Expansion, Contemporary Style

Many so-called modern houses look, when brand-new, as if they were made up of additions stitched together. Indeed, when the houses shown here—part of an unusual development of more than 400 small homes near Washington, D.C.—first were sold in 1949, the promotional brochure promised that "provision is made for future additional structures such as breezeways, carports, workshops and rooms for living." Since then, expansions have added dramatic beauty and extra space—and multiplied values many times over.

A two-story wing. The original house at the left below is overshadowed by the new wing, which enlarges one bathroom of the house and adds a large, two-story family room, two small upstairs bedrooms and an upstairs bathroom.

The original. Photographed in a way that emphasizes its similarity to the houses at bottom and right, this house has a simple floor plan: living room behind the porch at left, kitchen in the center and bedrooms to the right.

Additions to fit a lot. The locations of the new entryway at left and the tall studio/library behind it—the original structure stretches to the right—reflect a delicate compromise between zoning limitations on outward expansion and the owners' desire to preserve the garden of trees and specimen plants behind the house.

A classic entrance. A modernized version of the old-fashioned vestibule enables a guest to pause to orient himself; it also provides a gracious bridge between the original living room and the new wing and a passageway to the garden as well. The warm colors of the hand-made Mexican floor tiles and the exposed brick of the chimney provide a backdrop for clay planters made by one of the owners of the house.

How to Splice the New Roof onto the Old

The roof for a small one-story addition generally is built in one of two common forms: a shed roof, with a single sloping surface; or a gable roof, with two sloping surfaces that meet at a peak, or ridge. An architect can help you choose a roof for your addition, and will recommend a specific slope—that is, the inches of vertical rise per foot of horizontal run.

The slope is critical not only for practical reasons but also because it can make the difference between an ugly addition and an attractive one. For a shed roof, an architect is likely to recommend a gentle slope of 4 inches or less per foot of horizontal span; for a gable roof, a slope that matches that of the existing roof. (An easy method for measuring this slope is shown opposite, top.) These general rules must be adapted to special circumstances. In a gable roof fitted to a house wall, for example, clearing second-floor windows may require a shallow slope.

The type of roofing material you select may also affect the slope of your roof. Tile and slate cannot be used on a roof that slopes less than 4 inches in 12. Wood shingles and shakes need a minimum slope of 3 inches in 12, asphalt shingles and metal panels 2 inches in 12, while roll roofing requires only 1 inch in 12.

A shed roof is relatively easy to build. Rafters secured to the side of the house support the sheathing and roofing, and light joists support the new ceiling. If you like a high sloping ceiling or if you build a nearly flat roof, you can omit the joists.

A gable roof built against the side of a house is little more difficult than the shed type. In one respect, in fact, it is easier: because the span of each rafter is half the rafter span in a shed roof of the same size, you can use lighter lumber. But a gable roof always must have ceiling joists to keep the rafters from spreading apart at the bottom, and for a roof with a slope of less than 4 inches in 12, you may need additional braces called collar beams between pairs of rafters.

Joining a gable roof to the side of an existing roof presents special problems. The rafters between the old roof and the new ridge beam must be made progressively shorter up to the point where the two roofs meet. At their bases these short rafters, called jack rafters, must be set back from the joint between the old and new roofs, and must be cut at a specified angle to match the roof slope (chart, below). In addition, the eaves of the new roof must both meet and blend with those of the existing structure.

Blending eaves is primarily a matter of duplicating the detail work of the cornice—that is, the trim of the eaves—in the existing house (two common types are shown opposite). Making eaves meet at the same level, so that the roofs of both the addition and the main house appear to have a single continuous eave, is trickier if the rafters of the addition are narrower than those of the main roof.

In such a roof with an overhang of at least 12 inches, the discrepancy can be corrected by making a shorter overhang on the addition (page 61, Step 7). For roofs with little or no overhang, professional carpenters use a variety of methods to raise the addition rafters to the level of the main rafters at the eaves. Some alter the angle cuts, called bird's-mouths, of the addition rafters to match the heel—the vertical distance above the eave wall—of addition and main rafters. Others raise addition rafters by installing extra top plates or thin shims between rafters and wall. For amateurs the best method is to avoid the problem entirely by making the addition rafters of the same size lumber as the main rafters.

Fitting the Rafters to the Roof

| Roof slope | Height of vertical end cuts in common lumber sizes | | | | | Jack rafters | |
	2 × 4	2 × 6	2 × 8	2 × 10	2 × 12	Setback	Foot angle
1″	3½″	5½″	7¼″	9¼″	10¼″	4¼″	5°
2″	3½″	5½″	7⅜″	9⅜″	11⅜″	2⅛″	10°
3″	3⅝″	5⅝″	7½″	9½″	11⅝″	1⅜″	15°
4″	3¾″	5¾″	7⅝″	9¾″	11⅞″	1″	19°
5″	3¾″	6″	7⅞″	10″	12¼″	⅞″	23°
6″	3⅞″	6⅛″	8⅛″	10⅜″	12⅝″	¾″	27°
7″	4″	6⅜″	8⅜″	10¾″	13″	⅝″	31°
8″	4¼″	6⅝″	8¾″	11⅛″	13½″	½″	34°
9″	4⅜″	6⅞″	9″	11½″	14″	½″	37°
10″	4½″	7⅛″	9⅜″	12″	14⅝″	½″	40°
11″	4¾″	7⅜″	9¾″	12½″	15¼″	⅜″	43°
12″	5″	7¾″	10¼″	13″	15⅞″	⅜″	45°

Data for making addition rafters. This table provides specifications essential to the pages that follow, organized according to rafter slopes, which are given as inches of rise per foot of span. It lists heights of the angled end cuts of five sizes of rafters so that, by using the figure for the size and slope of your rafters, you can determine where to place a rafter plate (page 58, Step 1) or a ridge beam (page 59, Step 1).

The last two columns apply to jack rafters, short rafters that support an addition roof wherever it overlaps the main roof. One column indicates setback, the placement relative to a chalk line of these rafters and the plate that supports them (page 60, Step 3); the other indicates the angle at which to set the blade of a circular saw to fit the foot of a jack rafter to the roof beneath it (page 61, Step 5).

Measuring a roof slope. Mark the top of a level 12 inches from one end, set that end against the underside of a rafter inside the attic or a rake board outside the house and, with the level horizontal, set a ruler or carpenter's square vertically at the mark. The distance in inches between the top of the level and the underside of the rafter or rake board is the rise of the roof in a 12-inch unit of run; in this example, the reading indicates a slope of 6 inches in 12.

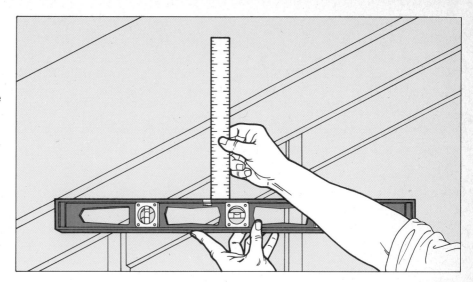

Two Basic Cornice Styles

A closed cornice. This relatively simple assembly creates a roof without an overhanging eave. After the roof sheathing has been installed, a plywood filler strip is nailed to the vertical ends—called the heels—of the rafters. A frieze board is nailed to the filler strip, and metal drip-edge flashing is fastened over the frieze. The gable edges are finished with a spacer board nailed to the edge of the roof, and a rake board, the same width as the frieze, nailed to the spacer.

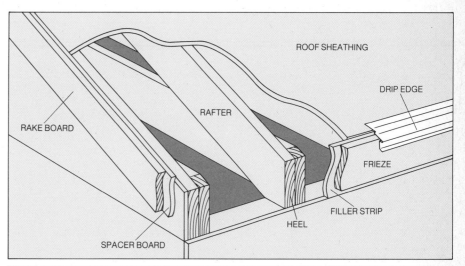

A box cornice. In this style the rafters project to frame an overhang at the eaves. A notch called a bird's-mouth near the end of each rafter fits the rafter to the top and outer edge of the top plate; the end of the rafter is cut vertically, the lower corner horizontally. A fascia and a drip edge cover the ends of the rafters, a plywood soffit protects the undersides, and a frieze board covers sheathing beneath the soffit. The rakes are treated as in the closed cornice described above, except that the lower end of the rake board has specially cut pieces (including a final piece called a pork chop) over the cornice end.

In a wide box cornice (*inset*) horizontal members called lookouts are set between rafter ends and sheathing to frame and support the soffit.

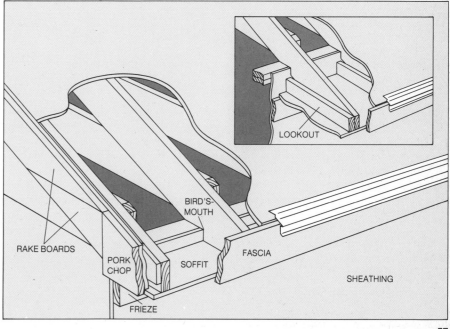

Building a Shed Roof

1 Mounting the plates. Attach plates for ceiling joists and rafters to the house, cutting both plates to the distance between the outer edges of the top plates on the addition side walls. Make the joist plate of lumber the same size as the joists, and set it on the side-wall top plates. Make the rafter plate as wide as the vertical end cut for the size and slope of your rafters (*chart, page 56*). To set the height of the top of this plate above the side-wall top plates, subtract 5½ inches from the length of a side wall, divide by 12 and multiply by the roof slope (for example, if the slope is 4 in 12, multiply by 4); then add the figure for the vertical end cut.

In a frame wall, nail the plates, then screw lag bolts through them into the studs. In masonry, drill holes in the plates to guide you in drilling into mortar joints for bolts and lead anchors.

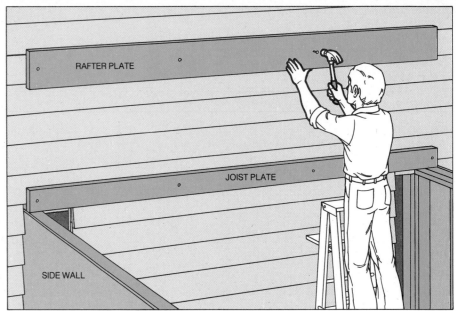

2 Hanging the joists. Fasten metal joist hangers to the face of the joist plate at 2-foot intervals, beginning 1½ inches from one end and setting the bottom strap of each hanger flush with the bottom of the plate. Position the last hanger 1½ inches from the other end of the plate. Fasten metal joist anchors atop the outer wall of the addition in corresponding positions, then cut and install the ceiling joists.

3 Hanging the rafters. Nail a length of rafter stock temporarily to the side of the addition and the end of the rafter plate, setting its position by the following method. Trim the upper end of the rafter at an angle roughly estimated to make it rest against both the house wall and the end of the rafter plate. Align the rafter with the upper edge of the upper end flush with the top of the rafter plate, and the lower edge of the other end aligned with the inner edge of the end-wall top plate (*inset*). On the temporarily nailed rafter, trace around the end wall for the bird's-mouth cut; trace the rafter plate at the other end for an accurate angle cut. Mark the outer edge of the rafter for the cornice style you have chosen. Cut the rafter at the marks and use it as a template for the other rafters.

Set the first rafter alongside the first joist, flush with the side wall; nail the rafter to the joist, and use metal plates to fasten it to the top and rafter plates. Install the remaining rafters 2 feet apart except for the last one, which—like the first—should be flush with the side wall.

4 **Installing cripple studs.** Cut 2-by-4 studs to fit at 16-inch intervals between the outermost rafters and the side-wall top plates with the wide sides of the studs facing outward, and toenail the studs to the rafters and the top plates. At the house wall, turn the studs so that the wide sides are resting flat against the wall, and nail the studs to the wall between the rafter and joist plates.

At the addition end wall, saw the corners of the joists flush with the upper edges of the rafters.

Building a Gable Roof

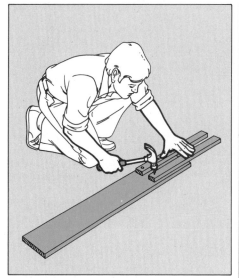

1 **Braces for a ridge beam.** Make two temporary supports for the ridge beam by nailing pairs of 1-by-2s 1½ inches apart to the ends of 2-by-6s cut to the height of the ridge beam above the addition walls. To calculate this height, subtract 9½ inches from the width of the addition and divide by 24. Multiply the result by the roof slope, then add the figure for the end cut of your rafters (*chart, page 56*). Finally, subtract the width of the ridge beam.

Install ceiling joists between the side walls of the addition, using metal anchors at 2-foot intervals and setting the outermost joists 1½ inches from the ends of the plates (*Step 2, opposite*). Nail and brace a ridge-beam support to the center of each outermost joist, placing the bottom of the support flush with the bottom of the joist. Cut a set of rafters (*Step 3, opposite*).

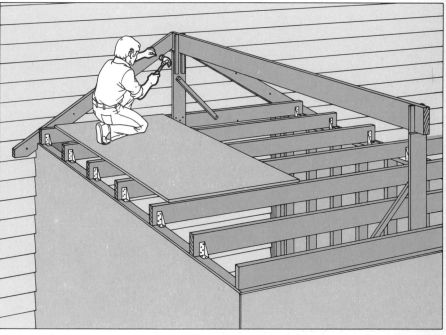

2 **Mounting the rafters.** Set the ridge beam in place; then, at the house wall, nail a pair of rafters in place atop the plates and against the ridge beam, and secure the rafters to the wall with bolts (*Step 1, opposite*). Mount the remaining pairs at 2-foot intervals, using nails at the joists and metal angle plates at the top plates and the ridge beam. Saw off the outer corners of the joists flush with the upper edges of the rafters; install cripple studs, cut to fit between the end-wall top plate and the end rafters, at the gable end of the addition roof (*Step 4, above*).

59

Intricate Angles of Intersecting Roofs

1 **Cutting the ridge beam.** Set a length of ridge-beam stock in temporary braces (*page 59, Step 1*). At the point where it touches the roof of the house, drive a marker nail down into the attic; then hold a board on the roof against the beam, and trace the roof slope onto the beam. Cut the beam to fit and mark it for rafters at 2-foot intervals; then set it back in place. If the point of the marker nail protrudes inside the attic between two rafters, install a bracing board of rafter stock between those rafters. On the roof, nail the end of the new ridge beam through the roof into a bracing board or a rafter.

2 **Installing rafters.** Cut pairs of rafters (*page 58, Step 3*), but for the main part of the roof, leave the rafter ends uncut and long enough to extend below the edge of the existing roof; for the position just outside the edge of the existing roof make the rafters 2 feet longer. If a rafter position falls inside the existing roof, trim the ends of this pair (*inset*) for a closed cornice as described on page 57, center. Install all but one pair of the rafters, starting at the gable end of the addition. Use a reserved rafter as a template for the end cuts of the jack rafters (*Steps 5 and 6, opposite*). Install cripple studs at the gable end of the addition (*page 59, Step 4*).

3 **Positioning roof plates.** With a helper, extend a chalk line from the point where the top of the ridge beam meets the main roof down over the tops of the long rafters on each side of the addition; the line should graze both the roof and the rafters. Snap this line on each side of the addition roof. Then snap a second line inside the first on each side; to find how far inside—the "setback" distance between the first and second lines—use the chart on page 56.

60

4 Installing the roof plates. Nail roof plates of ½-inch plywood, 12 inches wide, between the ridge beam and the cut edge of the main roof, aligning the outer edge of each plate with the second of the chalk lines made in Step 3. To mark the roof plates for the lower ends of the jack rafters, drop a plumb line from the rafter positions you marked along the ridge beam and, at the points where the plumb bob touches the existing roof, run horizontal lines on the roof to the roof plates.

5 A compound cut for a jack rafter. Using a template rafter reserved in Step 1, trace the horizontal cut of its bird's-mouth at the middle of a piece of rafter stock that is close to twice as long as the template (*right, top*). Extend the line across the stock. Set a circular saw to the angle required for your roof slope (*chart, page 56*) and cut along the marks (*right, bottom*), creating left- and right-hand pieces. Cut other jack rafters in the same way, estimating lengths approximately.

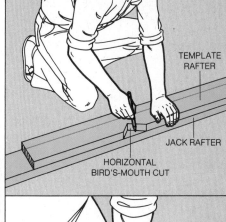

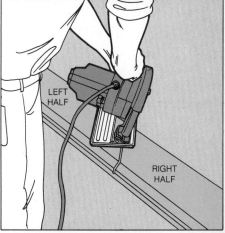

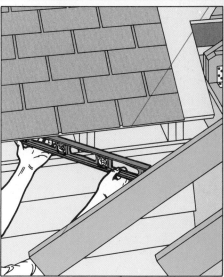

6 Completing jack rafters. With a tape, measure from the top of the ridge beam to the outer edge of the roof plate at each jack-rafter location. Mark this distance on each left-hand jack rafter cut in Step 5, measuring along the upper edge. Set the ridge end of a template rafter at this mark, aligning its longest edge with that of the jack rafter, trace the ridge cut of the template (*inset*), and saw the jack rafter there. Use the left-hand rafters as templates to mark ridge cuts on right-hand ones. Toenail the jack rafters to the roof plate and fasten them to the ridge beam with metal angle plates. Install the template rafters last.

7 Trimming the rafters. At each side of the addition, remove a short section of the fascia from the main roof of the house and set a level under the edge of the main-roof sheathing, then swing the level until its end touches the top of the nearest addition rafter. Mark that rafter at this point, cut it at the mark to match the ends of the main-roof rafters; cut the other addition rafters to match the first. To complete the framing, match the cornice trim of the addition to that of the main roof.

The Special Problems of an Extended Roof

A gabled addition at the gable end of a house has a unique roof design. Instead of running the addition roof into the side or roof of the main house, as on pages 59-61, the builder generally must extend the main roof to cover the addition. When the addition is as high and wide as the house, the entire roof is extended. When the addition has a front or back wall as high as that of the house, but is not as wide, an extension of the main roof is generally built at the front or back of the house; for the other half of the addition, a new roof is run into the side of the house *(right)*.

If the original main roof has an overhang at its gables, the addition will generally look best with a similar or identical overhang on the roof extension. Other problems arise when the addition is almost, but not quite, as wide as the main house. If you find that the new roof meets the rake trim of the old, remove the trim; flash the completed addition roof in the usual way *(pages 64-65),* and reinstall the trim over the flashing. If the new roof meets the old just under the rake trim, so that you do not have enough room to install roofing and flashing, extend the existing rake trim down onto the new roof and flash to it.

Two roof treatments. Because this addition has been built flush with the front of the main house but is set back at the rear, its roof is matched to the house in two different ways. At the front of the house, the main roof is extended to cover the addition; at the rear, the addition roof runs beneath the main roof and meets the house at the gable wall. If the addition were not set back at the rear of the house, the entire main roof would be extended to cover it.

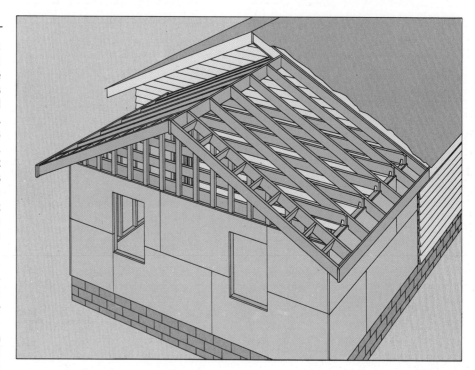

Setting the Ridge Beam, End Rafter and Overhang

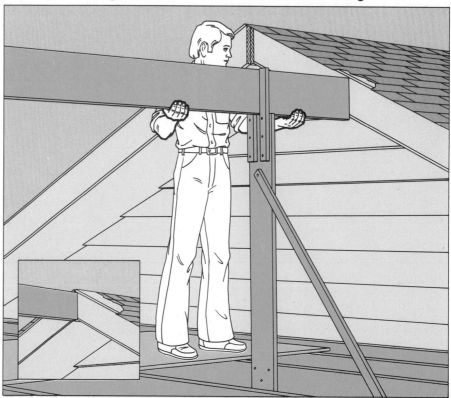

Putting up the ridge beam. Remove rake trim from the main roof—on one side for an extension of part of the roof; on both sides for a complete extension—and install joists and a ridge beam on the addition in the usual way *(page 59, Steps 1 and 2).* For the partial extension shown here, align the upper edge of the ridge with the upper edge of the end rafter. If you are extending both roof slopes, butt the new ridge beam to the end of the old one *(inset).* Fasten the new ridge beam to the end rafters of the main house with angle plates and nails.

Putting up the rafters. Install rafters on the addition (*page 58, Step 3*), starting at the gable end and, in this partial extension, fastening the innermost rafters to an end rafter and to the gable wall of the main house. If you are extending both slopes of the main roof, fasten the innermost addition rafters to the end rafters of the house. To set the slope of the rafter next to a gable wall, have a helper hold a perfectly straight board against the undersides of the installed rafters, and align the rafter with this board and with the top plate of the addition. Cut the upper end of this rafter to fit beneath the soffit board in the overhang trim of the main roof.

Although the addition roof will be sheathed and flashed in the usual way (*pages 64-65*), you must notch the sheathing to fit the overhang of the main roof. You need not fasten the sheathing to the soffit of the overhang, but you must install flashing along the joint between the sheathing and soffit and at the joint between the old rake and the new roof. Cover this rake flashing with new rake trim, installed between the peaks of the old and new roofs.

Building an overhang at the rake. Match the cornice trim of the addition to that of the main roof (*page 57*), but extend the fascia beyond the outermost rafter to the outer edge of the planned rake overhang. At this edge, install a rafter between the fascia and the ridge beam, then nail bracing blocks the same size as the rafters between the rake rafter and the outermost main rafter at 16-inch intervals.

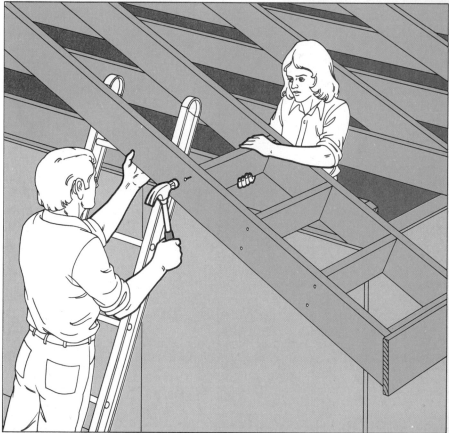

Finishing an Addition Roof

Roofing for an addition generally duplicates that on the existing house. In most cases it will consist of sheathing of ½-inch plywood; felt underlayment; flashing at edges and valleys, best made of aluminum, and the same shingles used for the house. However, if the roofing is shakes, you need sheathing of 1-by-3 slats; if the slope of the addition roof is less than 2 inches per foot, use roll roofing instead of shingles or shakes. Because all addition roofs must be flashed at newly created joints, most drawings on these pages concern flashing.

Matching new roofing material to old can be tricky. Old roofing changes color as it weathers. Also, you may encounter an odd installation pattern in asphalt shingles or in the depths of the courses in wooden shingles and shakes. If you cannot make a good match, it is best to reroof the main house.

On a small addition roof, gutters are not generally necessary. The exception is an intersecting gable roof, where there is a heavy flow of water from the valleys between the main and addition roofs. In this case, either extend the main-roof gutters around the addition (*opposite, bottom*) or install gutters on both roofs.

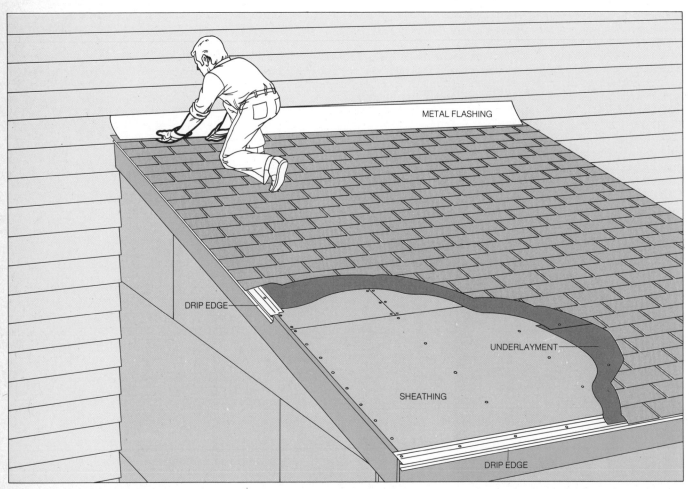

Flashing a shed roof. Sheathe the roof and add drip edges, underlayment and roofing. For clapboard siding, slip a strip of aluminum flashing up underneath the siding board just above the addition roof and bend the bottom of the strip to lap over the roof. Nail through the siding board and flashing at 12-inch intervals.

For plywood or vertical board siding, cut a 1-inch slot above the roof, install the flashing in the same way, and caulk the joint between the upper edge of the slot and the flashing.

In brick siding, use a circular saw with a masonry blade to cut a groove ½ inch deep into a horizontal mortar joint about 6 inches above the top of the roof. Install one strip of bent flashing flat to the wall and the roof, nailing it with masonry nails driven into mortar joints. Install a second strip—called counterflashing—into the groove, then bend it down over the first strip. Nail and caulk the counterflashing at the groove.

Flashing a gable roof at a wall. To seal the joints at the edge of this roof, small, individually cut rectangles of flashing are installed alternately with courses of roofing. Start the job by installing sheathing, drip edges and underlayment, with the underlayment lapped 3 inches up the adjoining wall. As you lay each course of roofing, cover at least 2 inches of its upper half with a rectangle of flashing cut to fit; bend the piece and set its upper edge under a clapboard, in a diagonal slot cut into plywood or vertical wooden siding, or under a piece of counterflashing on brick siding. In clapboard, caulk the vertical gaps between the flashing strips.

The flashing at the roof peak consists of two precut pieces: one folded over the ridge and extending up the wall on each side, the other piece extending down the wall over the first and notched to fit the roof peak.

Flashing an intersecting roof. A special type of valley flashing, shaped like a W in cross section and fitted with nailing cleats, protects the valleys between old and new roofs. Cut the existing roofing back 3 inches from the center of each valley and remove any nails within 7 inches of the centers; remove shingles directly above the peak of the addition roof to clear about 2 square feet of sheathing. Working from the addition side of each valley, slip the edges of the valley flashing underneath the edges of the existing roofing and nail the flashing to the roof through its cleats. Trim the flashing 1 foot above the peak of the valleys, hammer it flat to the roof, and replace the shingles you removed.

Running a Gutter around a Corner

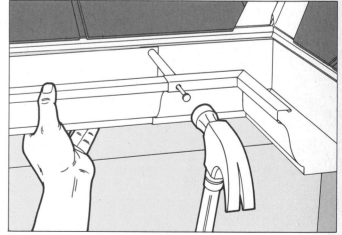

Adding the gutters. To reinstall the existing gutters, add a corner piece to each end that was cut away for the addition and extend the gutter along the new fascia to a downspout at the end of the wall. If water overflows the gutter at a valley, install an extra downspout there.

Inside the House: An Opening in the Common Wall

In most cases, the opening between an addition and the house—installed after the addition is roofed and weathertight—is easy to provide. It raises special problems in only one instance—an addition to the first floor of a two-story house that must be a seamless extension of an existing room, leaving walls and ceilings uninterrupted. Even then, the problem is solved simply in nonbearing walls; only a seamless opening that breaches a bearing wall (the front and back walls in most houses) requires the additional construction indicated in the drawing below.

Most additions, however, are not extensions but separate rooms. Entry can be provided by making use of an existing door, or if there is none, by converting an existing window or making an entirely new door or framed opening as described on page 46. Many extensions can be handled similarly—a wide framed opening serves well if the extension is meant to create space for a distinct purpose—to be a dining area, for example.

When the addition is used to expand a cramped room, an entire wall must be shifted. The shift may be slight—but a few feet added to the width of a long, narrow living room will improve its proportions, and 5 or 6 extra feet can convert a single bedroom into a comfortable double. In cases like these, a framed opening with its header beam visible just below ceiling level is objectionable. Such a construction can be avoided except when the opening is in a one-story house; in such a house there is no easy way to support the existing roof rafters except with a header that hangs beneath the existing ceiling.

To provide a seamless opening in a nonbearing wall of a two-story house, cut away part of the ceiling adjacent to it, revealing the ceiling joists, which run parallel to a nonbearing wall. Reinforce the stringer joist—the joist above the wall—by nailing to it a piece of ½-inch plywood and a board the same size as the joist. Then the wall can be removed.

How you provide a seamless opening in a bearing wall of a two-story house depends on the width of the opening. If the opening is more than 12 feet wide, a steel I-beam supported by steel pipe columns and reinforced foundation footings will be needed; such a job requires considerable experience in heavy construction, as well as the advice of a structural engineer.

For an opening less than 12 feet wide, however, you can reinforce the header joist to make it a substitute for the bearing wall. The existing header joist sits atop the existing bearing wall, and the ceiling joists, revealed when the adjacent ceiling sections are removed, run perpendicular to it. The reinforcement is made by bolting a ⅜-inch steel plate and another joist alongside the original one, as described on these pages.

Before you order the steel plate, make a diagram showing where each ceiling joist meets the header joist. Use this diagram to prepare a guide for the steel supplier to follow in drilling the boltholes. They should fall between joists in the pattern required by the local building code—holes every 8 inches, staggered 2 inches from the top and bottom, are usually sufficient.

Because the ceiling joists meet the inside face of the existing header joist, the reinforcement must be bolted to the outside face. If you are using a shed roof—usual for a room extension—install the roof rafters in the normal way (page 58, Steps 1-3), but do not add ceiling joists to the addition until you have finished the opening. You then can fasten both the original ceiling joists and the ceiling joists of the addition to the reinforced header joist, using steel brackets.

Supports for a seamless opening. In a two-story house, the weight of the second floor—formerly supported by a bearing wall—is carried by a header joist reinforced with a steel plate and a 2-inch board. The ends of the joists, which had rested on the top plate of the old bearing wall, are supported by steel joist hangers. The ends of the reinforced header are supported by posts made from 2-by-4s.

This method cannot be used to replace a bearing wall more than 12 feet wide. Nor does it serve in a one-story house; there the supporting header must be below ceiling level.

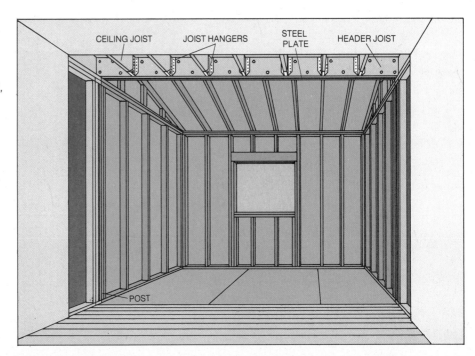

A Hidden Header for a Seamless Ceiling

1 **Removing the wallboard.** Support the second floor with temporary shoring *(page 28, Step 1)*, remove the studs and sole plate of the existing wall, then saw horizontally along the side-wall covering on each side of the opening, cutting through the wall covering until you hit a stud. Next, saw vertically along the stud, cutting from floor to ceiling, and remove the section of side-wall covering next to the opening. Snap a chalk line across the ceiling, in line with the studs that you have revealed; saw along the line and remove the covering of the ceiling.

2 **Prying out the last studs.** If a corner stud remaining from the old wall protrudes at each side of the opening, pry it away from the side-wall studs behind it, starting at the bottom and working up. Cut off the piece of sole plate that is left beneath the stud, using a handsaw, and pry it up from the floor. (For clarity, the temporary shoring shown in Step 1 has been omitted here.)

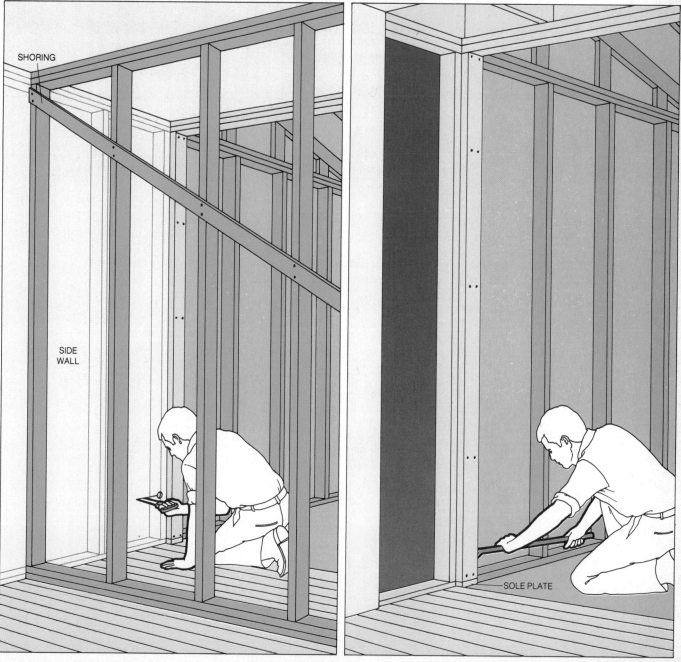

SHORING

SIDE WALL

SOLE PLATE

3 **Removing the top plates.** Cut the double top plates of the old wall flush with the side walls, using the side-wall studs as a guide; be careful not to saw into the header joist. Wedge a pry bar between the upper top plate and the bottom of each joist; pry the plates away and knock them free with a sledge hammer.

Reinforce the connection between the addition wall and the existing side wall (*page 47, Step 4*) by driving staggered 16-penny nails through the end studs of the addition wall every 6 inches.

4 **Supporting the header joist.** Cut a stud ⅛ inch longer than the studs in the addition walls and hammer it tight against the end stud. Nail the new stud to the end stud with staggered 16-penny nails every 6 inches and toenail it to the top and sole plates. Build a post at the other edge of the opening in the same way.

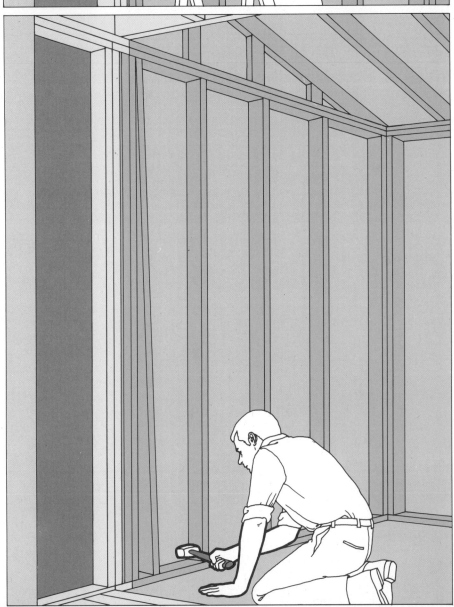

5 **Reinforcing the header joist.** Align the predrilled steel plate on top of a 2-inch board that is as wide as the header joist and long enough to span the top plates of the addition walls. Using the steel plate as a template, drill matching holes through the board.

With a helper, set the steel plate on the top plates, alongside the header joist, and use it as a template to drill matching holes in this joist.

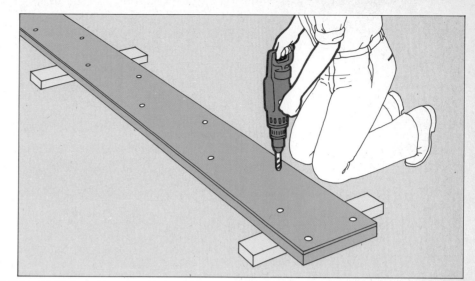

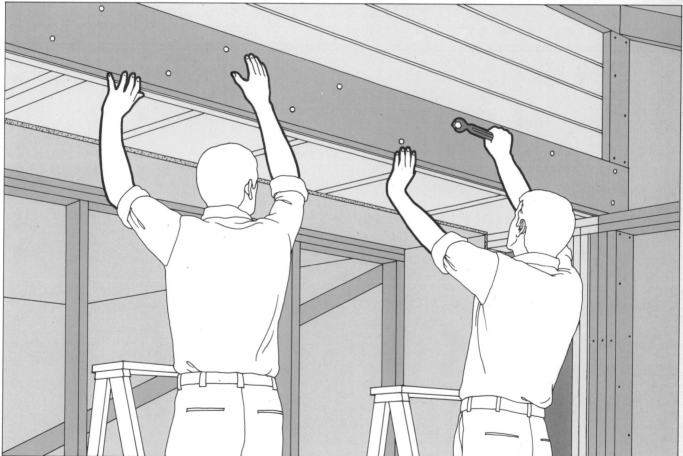

6 **Bolting the header together.** Set the drilled board beside the plate. Bolt the drilled board, the plate and the header joist together with machine bolts, large washers and nuts. Toenail each end of the drilled board to the top plate. Nail metal hangers to the existing ceiling joists and to the header joist. Install the ceiling joists of the addition (page 58, Step 2) and fasten them to the header joist with joist hangers.

Simple Wiring for a Small Addition

Any addition to your home—even one as small as a bay window—probably must be supplied with electricity. Electrical codes commonly require receptacles every 12 feet. You may also wish to install a ceiling light or electric heating.

How much power you need and where you get it depends in part on your addition and in part on the current available in your house. A small addition that can be heated by the house furnace may require as few as three receptacles. If a nearby house circuit is not heavily used, you can extend it to the addition. But do not put more than a total of 12 outlets on a 15-ampere circuit or more than 16 on a 20-ampere circuit.

If the power required exceeds these limitations, you need a new circuit. Install a 15- or 20-ampere circuit for lights and a 20-ampere circuit for small appliances and for each permanently installed unit, such as an electric heater or room air conditioner, that is rated at 1400 watts or more. (In Canada, most household wiring circuits are 15 amperes.)

If the existing service panel has space for new circuit breakers or fuses, you can add simple circuits as shown on these and the following pages. But before doing so, calculate the total electrical load of your existing house in watts and amperes to be sure you have enough unused power coming into the service panel. If you do not, install a new panel for a larger load. If the panel has adequate capacity but there is no room in it for a new circuit, install a subpanel for the addition.

To help plan circuits and wire them, draw a plan of your addition, showing locations of electrical boxes and devices as well as routes for wires. You may have to submit this plan when you apply for an electrical permit but you can also use

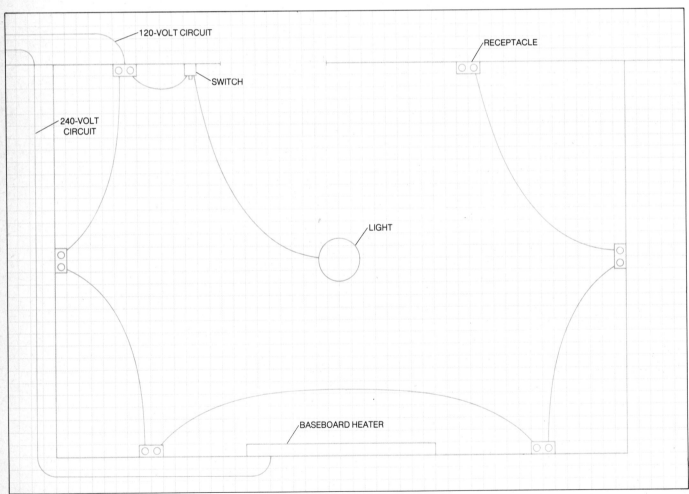

Mapping circuits. On a plan of your addition, mark the location of each switch, receptacle, lighting fixture and electric heater. Then draw the routes of the cables between the connections for use as a guide in wiring the circuits. This diagram shows two circuits. One, a 240-volt circuit, goes to a baseboard heater with an internal thermostat. The other, a 120-volt lighting circuit, enters the addition at a receptacle near the door, where it splits. One run goes to the receptacles, the other run goes to an overhead light controlled by a switch at the door.

it as a shopping list to buy materials. For example, you need a standard rectangular outlet box 2½ inches deep for most connections that call for two cables with 12-gauge copper wires; for three cables buy a rectangular box 3½ inches deep; for four, a 4-inch square box. Use boxes with hanger bars for positions between studs or joists. Estimate two jumper-wire connections and three or four wire caps per box. When buying switches, be sure you get a model with a grounding screw installed by the manufacturer.

Begin wiring your addition when it is weathertight—with sheathed walls and roof and installed doors and windows—but before insulation or wallboard is installed. New wiring must pass two inspections. For the first one, called a rough-in inspection, mount wall and ceiling boxes, placing them so that they will be flush with the finished surface. Most electric heaters need no wiring box, since the unit's housing serves this function.

After installing the boxes, run cable—with 14-gauge copper wire for 15-ampere circuits, 12-gauge for 20-ampere circuits—from the service panel into the addition, then to each box and to each heater location in turn. Make up the ground connections in each box and call the electrical inspector for the rough-in inspection. The inspector will check cable support, ground connections, and the path of each circuit from the service panel to its endpoint in the addition.

The final inspection occurs after you have laid finish flooring, installed wallboard and sanded the joints. At this time, wire the switches, receptacles and light fixtures, secure them in the boxes, and screw on the cover plates. Install and wire electric baseboard heaters.

The last step is to make the connections at the service panel. Before starting this part of the job, have the power company shut off the power to the service panel. When all of the connections are completed, have the electrical power restored and make arrangements for the final inspection.

Mounting Outlet Boxes

Nailing a box to the framing. A box with a cleated flange is the easiest type to install in addition framing. First mark the height of a box on a stud. Align the box so that the flange is flush with the edge of the stud. Tap the cleats into the stud to hold the box in position while you nail it. Receptacles are commonly set 12 inches above the floor, wall switches 48 inches, but position them to suit your needs. For an overhead light, round or octagonal boxes with side-mounted flanges can be fastened to a joist; or boxes can be screwed to hanger bars if you need to mount them in positions between joists *(inset)*.

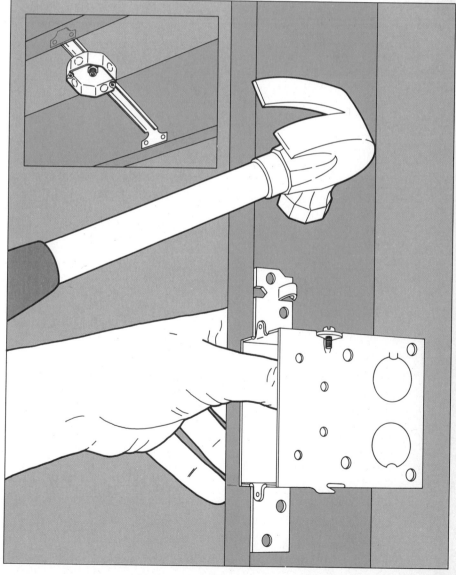

Running Cable from the House to the Addition

Holes through studs and joists. Following your circuit plan, drill ¾-inch holes at a convenient height through the centers of studs or joists. Electrical codes usually require that holes be at least 1¼ inches from the edges of framing members; drilling through centers is preferable.

Wiring the addition from below. In an addition with a crawl space, drill a hole through the sole plate and subflooring near the first box on the circuit. Then drill a second hole through the end or header joists of the house and the addition (*inset*). This hole is most easily drilled from the house basement, if there is one.

Fish cables from the service panel—leaving a 2-foot tail of cable for the service-panel connections—through the holes and into the addition. No special support is necessary for cable that runs horizontally through holes drilled in studs or joists; otherwise, anchor cable with staples or clamps no more than 4½ feet apart.

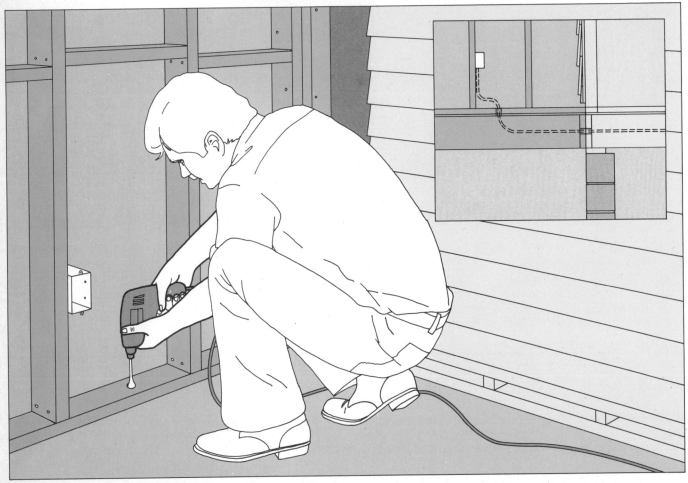

Wiring the addition from above. Drill through the top plates of the addition and the exterior house wall. If you are drilling into an unfinished attic, it does not matter where you drill through the wall. If you are drilling into a finished second floor, drill through the wall into the cavity around plumbing pipes—if they are nearby—or into a closet. If neither is available, drill into an interior wall; then, from the attic, drill down through the top plate into the wall (*inset*).

Any of the methods described allows you to avoid fishing cable through the exterior walls, which in most cases are full of obstructions. Pull cable from the service panel, across the attic and into the addition, supporting the cable as described (*opposite, bottom*).

Wiring the Boxes

Fastening cables to boxes. With a screwdriver, remove a knockout for each cable in a box. Remove 8 inches of cable sheathing with a utility knife and ½ inch of insulation from the ends of the wires, then clamp the cable in the box. Secure the cable to the framing with a staple or clamp within 12 inches of the box.

To secure a cable in a junction box, since these come without clamps, use the two-part connector shown in the inset.

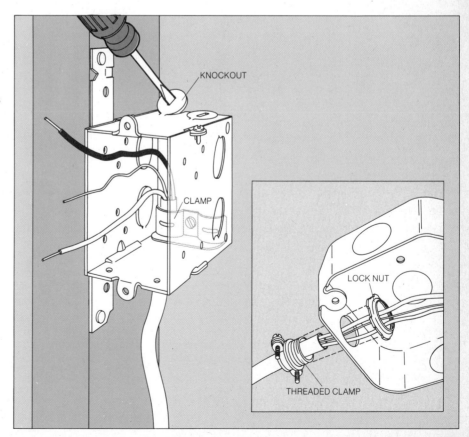

KNOCKOUT

CLAMP

LOCK NUT

THREADED CLAMP

Grounding boxes. For a switch or a receptacle, join two green jumper wires to the bare cable wires with a wire cap; connect one jumper to the box ground screw and save the other for later attachment to the grounding terminal—usually green—of the receptacle or switch. No jumper wire is needed for a light fixture, but one is necessary to connect cable wires if more than one cable enters the box. After making the ground connections, fold all the wires neatly and push them into the box.

Prewired electric baseboard heaters require no ground connections. To prepare for the rough-in inspection, simply bend an 8-inch tail of cable into the room so that the cable will not be covered when the walls are finished.

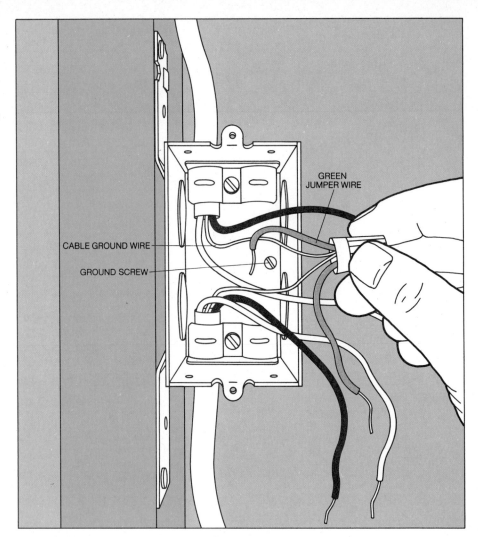

GREEN JUMPER WIRE

CABLE GROUND WIRE

GROUND SCREW

Making Power Connections

Attaching electrical devices. After wallboard has been installed, connect the free wires in the boxes to the devices. For a 240-volt electric heater, clamp the cable to the built-in box with a two-part connector, then mount the unit on the wall. Connect the black wire of the cable to either of the heater's two black wires with a wire cap; connect the white cable wire, after recoding it by painting or taping the end of it black, to the other black wire. Fasten the bare cable wire to the grounding screw in the heater box.

Connect light fixtures, receptacles and switches, observing the rule that black wires are attached to black wires or brass terminal screws; white wires, to white wires or silver terminal screws; and bare or green wires, to green terminal screws. Screw the devices into the boxes and conceal the boxes with cover plates.

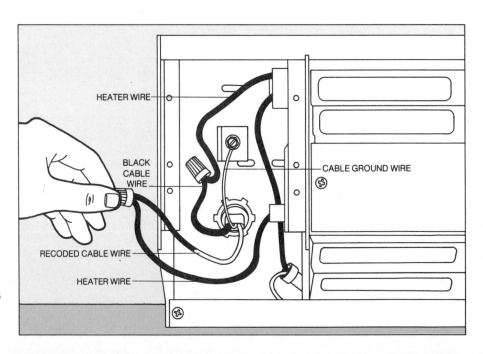

HEATER WIRE

BLACK CABLE WIRE

CABLE GROUND WIRE

RECODED CABLE WIRE

HEATER WIRE

Grounding the system. After having the power to the panel cut off and turning off the main circuit breaker or removing the main fuses, open a knockout for each new circuit. Pull the cables into the service panel and secure them with two-part clamps. Screw the bare wires and white wires of 120-volt circuits to the service panel's ground/neutral bar. Connect the bare wire of a 240-volt cable to the bar.

Caution: Do not connect the recoded white wire of any 240-volt circuit to the ground/neutral bar.

MAIN CIRCUIT BREAKER

GROUND/NEUTRAL BAR

240-VOLT CIRCUIT

120-VOLT CIRCUIT

Installing the circuit breakers. For a 120-volt circuit, snap a single-pole circuit breaker into the service panel and fasten the black wire to the terminal screw. For a 240-volt circuit, snap a double-pole circuit breaker into the clips in the service panel and screw the black wire to one terminal, the recoded white wire to the other.

In a fuse box, connect the black wire of the 120-volt circuit to the terminal screw of a fuse holder for a plug-type fuse; connect the black wire of a 240-volt circuit to one of the two terminal screws of a cartridge-fuse pull-out block and connect the recoded white wire to the other.

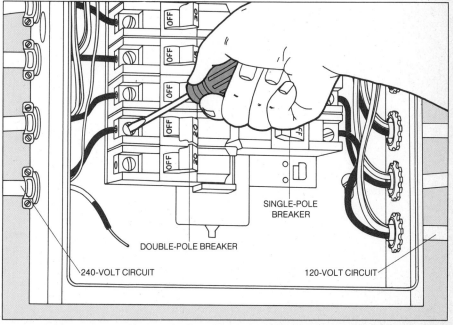

SINGLE-POLE BREAKER

DOUBLE-POLE BREAKER

240-VOLT CIRCUIT

120-VOLT CIRCUIT

Stealing Excess Heat to Warm an Addition

To heat an addition to your house, you can either extend the heating system you already have or install a new, independent system. You can do either job yourself, but you should have a professional heating contractor help you plan it. For a fee, he will analyze your existing system, advise you on the heating equipment you need and suggest the simplest and most efficient method of installation.

If your house has steam heat or gravity hot-air heat, he will probably advise you not to extend the pipes or ducts—normally, the entire system would need re-planning—but instead to install electric heaters in the addition. If your heating system uses forced hot water or air, you probably can extend it to an addition—the average American house furnace is at least 20 per cent bigger than it need be.

How you add on to a hot-water system depends on the type you have. In a one-pipe system, the most common, you must break into a single main pipeline for a pipe route called an extension loop, tapping into the line with riser pipes at each new convector. One end of the loop taps water from the main; the other returns the water to the main. In a two-pipe system, you must reroute two mains, and connect each convector to both of the rerouted mains.

In both systems, the crucial passage between the main house and the addition can be made through small holes bored in a header joist (page 72, bottom).

To minimize work with a propane torch in a cramped addition crawl space, assemble most of the extensions at a workbench. The final connections and the addition of insulation (page 124) can be made as a single final step of the job.

To extend a forced-air system, use round duct rather than rectangular, unless you plan to run part of the new branch within a wall. Wall installations are tricky—you must leave or make a gap in the subfloor and sole plate to run the duct, and exterior walls with insulation and firestops present special problems. Whatever type of duct you use, you will encounter one minor problem and, in some cases, a major one. The minor problem is the connection between the existing house and the addition; an air duct is too big to pass through a header joist, and you will have to make a hole in the masonry foundation for it. The major problem is assuring sufficient air flow into an addition located relatively far from the furnace.

If you have lived in your house for some time, you probably know where the system delivers too much or too little warm (or cool) air. An addition located alongside part of the house that already is undersupplied is likely to prove difficult to incorporate into the existing forced-air system.

The problem usually can be solved unless the added ducting turns. Keep it as straight as possible; if too many turns are necessary, extension may be impractical.

Several steps help achieve maximum air flow. If at all possible, attach the extension supply duct to the main supply duct of the existing system—tapping an individual room duct generally works only for a small addition. Provide return ducting as well as supply, although where you tap into the existing return duct is not critical for return.

Dampers located where ducts branch off the main duct also help, enabling you to divert air from oversupplied rooms. Dampers are lacking in many recently installed systems, but they are easy to put in and they greatly simplify the task of balancing a forced-air system for even heating of the entire house.

More direct boosting of air flow is also possible. The easiest way is to increase the speed of the furnace blower. On most recent models, speed is adjusted with a switch or by changing wire connections. And on any belt-driven blower, speed can be increased by changing pulley sizes—replacing the motor pulley with a bigger size or the fan pulley with a smaller size. If the furnace blower is already operating at the maximum desirable speed—very high speeds cause objectionable noise in the ducts—you can install an inexpensive booster fan inside the addition duct. Available at almost any hardware store, such a unit is wired in parallel with the furnace blower so that the two operate together.

Extending a Hot-Water System

1 **Joining extension sections.** For each new convector in a one-pipe system, solder an ordinary T to the extension piping at the point where the supply riser will be located. Solder a Venturi T (a fitting with a conical interior that boosts water pressure) for the return riser, setting the narrow end of the interior cone in the direction of water flow. Solder risers to both Ts.

For a two-pipe system, use two extensions—one from the supply main and one from the return—and solder ordinary Ts to both of the extensions for the riser connections.

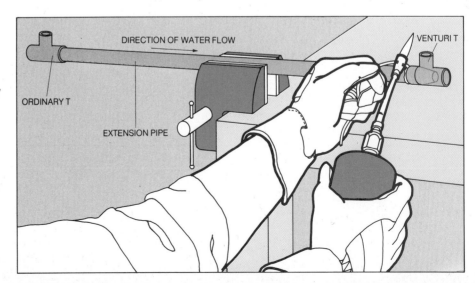

DIRECTION OF WATER FLOW

VENTURI T

ORDINARY T

EXTENSION PIPE

2 **Installing a convector.** After securing the back panel of the convector to studs in the addition wall, install the fittings of the heating element—an angle valve at the supply end, an elbow with vent tapping on the return end—and set the element in its mounting brackets. Drill riser holes through the floor under the fittings.

Install the extension piping under the floor, hanging the piping from the floor joists with metal straps, and run riser pipes from the extension up through the holes under the convector. Drill holes through the header joist of the main house, run the ends of the extension to the line or lines in the basement, and join any unsoldered connections of the extension.

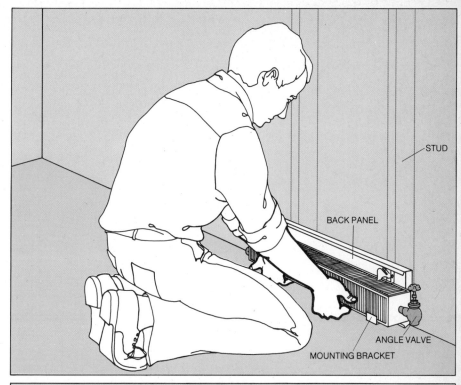

STUD

BACK PANEL

ANGLE VALVE

MOUNTING BRACKET

3 **Linking the convector to the pipes.** Place asbestos shields behind and under the convector to protect the wall and floor from the torch flame, and solder the joints between the heating element, the fittings and the risers.

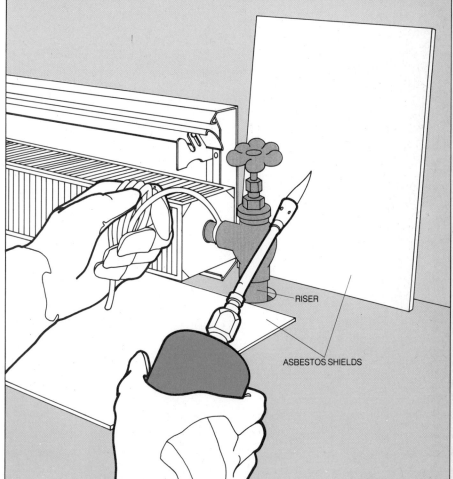

RISER

ASBESTOS SHIELDS

4 **Draining the system.** When weather permits you to shut down the heating system of the main house for several hours or more, turn off power to the boiler and shut the water-supply valve. Run a hose from the boiler drain cock to a drain and open the drain cock to let the water flow out of the system. Open the bleeder valves of all convectors located above the level of the boiler.

DRAIN COCK

WATER-SUPPLY VALVE

5 **Rerouting the main line.** Cut out the section of the main line between the two ends of the extension loop or pipes protruding through the header joist and, at each end of the cut main, attach a 90° elbow to turn the main upward, and a short section of pipe to raise it to the level of the extension piping. Use another 90° elbow to turn the main toward the extension piping and, if necessary, another short pipe with a slip coupling to connect into the extension.

To refill the system, reverse the sequence of Step 4: first close the convector bleeder valves and the boiler drain cock, then open the water-supply valve and, finally, restore power to the boiler.

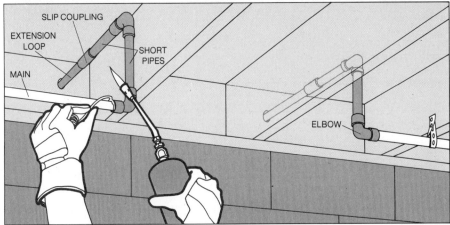

SLIP COUPLING

EXTENSION LOOP

SHORT PIPES

MAIN

ELBOW

Extending a Forced-Air System

1 **Assembling the duct extension.** Wear gloves to protect your hands against sharp edges when joining sections of duct. Slip the plain end of one section over the crimped end of another, punch or drill a hole through both sections on each side of the joint and fasten the sections together with sheet-metal screws. Cover the joint with duct tape. You will use a 90° angle boot to turn the end of the extension up to a register in the floor. Turns—there should be as few as possible—can be made with simple elbows or short sections of flexible duct.

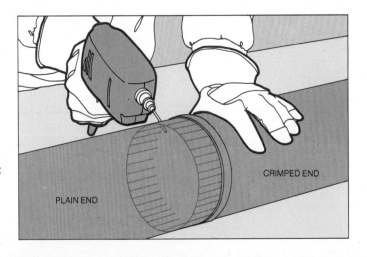

PLAIN END

CRIMPED END

2 **Cutting a path into the addition.** To run the duct extension from the main house into the space under the addition, chisel out a hole the size of the duct through the foundation wall; position the hole just under the sill plate and between two floor joists.

Fasten sheet-metal trim collars to both sides of the hole, using masonry nails; run the duct through the collars (*inset*) and hang it from the floor joists with metal straps.

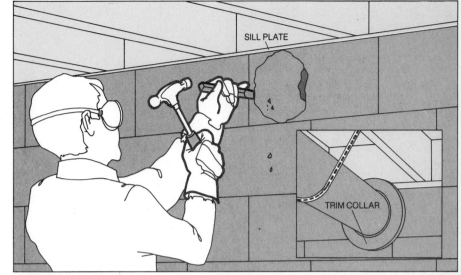

3 **Completing the duct run in the addition.** Working underneath the addition floor, mark the opening for a floor register on the underside of the addition subfloor, using the rectangular end of a 90° register boot as a template. Drill holes at the corners of the outline and cut the opening out from above. Bend the flanges of the boot flat, insert the boot through the hole and nail it to the floor. Fasten the round end of the boot to the end of the duct run.

Install a return the same way. If you need more than one register and return to supply your addition, run separate ducts for each.

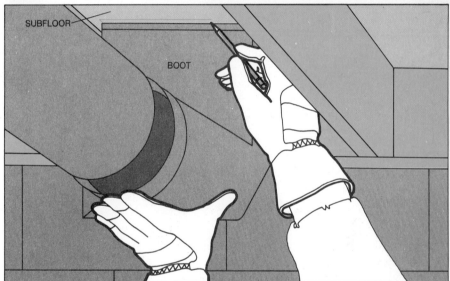

4 **Tapping into the main duct.** Turn off the furnace and, using the rectangular end of a take-off collar as a template, mark and cut out an opening in the main duct. Push the tabs of the collar into the opening you have cut and fold them back against the inside of the duct, then drill or punch holes through the flanges of the collar and fasten it to the duct with sheet-metal screws. Fasten the round end of the take-off collar to the first section of the duct run.

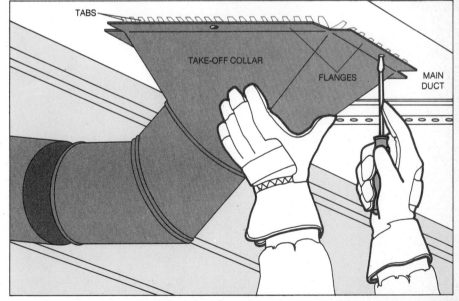

3 Putting On a Second Story

A jungle gym for safety. A framework of rented scaffolding, assembled in tiers, provides a safe platform for work high above the ground. The end sections, each 5 feet high, fit one atop the other so that any reasonable height can be reached. Bolted crossbars provide rigidity, but even so, any very tall scaffolding must be secured to the house with window or wall braces (*page 82*).

When expanding outward seems impractical—because your lot is too small or too hilly, or because a garden or a favorite tree is in the way—you can take advantage of what real estate dealers call air rights, the expanse of space stretching above your property. And by building new walls and a roof on top of a house or a garage, you make an addition that may be more economical to build than an equivalent ground structure would be.

Building above an existing foundation eliminates the heavy work and cost of making a new one. Many first-floor ceiling joists are strong enough to support a second floor, and sheathing from the old roof can be used as subflooring for the new floor. Extending utilities upward into an addition is generally less trouble than extending them horizontally—especially in homes built on slabs, where plumbing, heating and electrical lines may be encased in concrete.

In some cases you can double your floor space by adding an entire second story (*pages 132-133*), but most upward additions are more limited. Generally, the expansion involves either a shed dormer to make headroom in an attic, or a second story over the top of a garage. Both are equally suited to the most common purpose of all additions—to provide new bedrooms flanked by baths—and both could accommodate kitchens, airy studios, or upstairs living rooms.

Either type of addition raises two tricky problems for planners and builders. The first involves a stairway. Unless you have a full stairway to the attic—the retractable "disappearing stair" commonly found in one-story houses is unsatisfactory if the attic is to be used for any purpose but storage—you will have to install stairs to reach a shed dormer. You may be able to put them into halls or high stair wells above existing stairs, between first and second floors or between first floor and basement. Otherwise, you must rearrange existing rooms to accommodate stairs. For a garage-top addition the problem is simple because stairs inside the house are generally unnecessary; you can build them inside or outside the garage (*pages 100-109*).

The second problem involves work high aboveground. Nailing down the bottom of the new stairs is about the only work on an upward addition that can be done at ground level; the rest of the job takes place at least 10 feet higher, and falls are a hazard not to be shrugged off. To do the work safely, rent roof jacks and ladder hooks that make for sure footing on roofs, and erect scaffolding alongside walls. When you build a second story atop a garage, the new subfloor becomes a work platform on which to build and erect the new walls and roof. Moreover, the subfloor offers a convenient stacking space for materials so that a building supplier can use a crane on his truck to deliver lumber directly to the second story.

Room at the Top: A Shed Dormer for an Attic

If the roof of your house is held up by rafters, not trusses, and if the ridge beam is 10½ feet or more above the attic floor, you own a house suited to the addition of a shed dormer. Unlike a gable dormer, which brings light into an attic room but does not increase usable floor space very much, a shed dormer can convert an attic from a cramped storage space into a commodious area for several rooms. It can be almost as long as the ridge beam of the house, an expansion that is practical even if your house fills its lot.

The most popular style of shed dormer (*opposite, top*) begins at the roof ridge and extends all the way to the outside wall of the house to make the most of available space. This style also is the easiest to build. However, the procedure for constructing it, detailed on these and the following pages, can be adapted for a dormer that runs as much as 12 feet along the roof, with its front wall set back from the house wall and its roof beginning below the house ridge. Such a dormer may look more attractive, but it is less spacious and it requires shoring for the existing roof, which must be opened at an early stage, exposing the attic to rain.

To plan a dormer, first compare the span of the attic floor joists to their depth. If the joists are not big enough (a 2-by-6 joist can span 8 feet; a 2-by-8, 11 feet), you will have to double them (*page 94*). Locate the dormer so that it extends over the stairway in the house and, if you plan to put in a kitchen or bath, over the plumbing below (*page 120*). Each side of the dormer wall must rest directly on a rafter—any rafter but the end ones. If the dormer is more than half the roof length, or comes closer to the end rafter than a sixth of the roof length, you must build a bearing wall beneath the roof ridge.

In building the dormer, you and a helper will have to work on the roof and as high as 8 feet above the eaves. Secure your roof ladder not only with ladder hooks at the ridge but also with ropes tied to window braces on the other side of the house. To move across the roof, use roof jacks—adjustable supports for a 2-by-10 platform. For working above the eaves, use metal scaffolding, which comes in sections 5 feet high, 5 feet wide and up to 10 feet long.

Ready-made Scaffolds for Safety on High

Raising the sections. Set the legs of two end frames into base plates equipped with adjusting screws and rest them on 2-by-12 sills. Bolt two crosspieces in place, then level and plumb the section with the adjusting screws. Install a coupling pin at each corner of the section, then assemble a second section atop the first, keeping it level and plumb. To erect higher sections and to climb the completed scaffold, use the rungs of the end frames. Hook a set of special aluminum-and-plywood planks across the top of the scaffolding to make a work platform. Then install a double guardrail, leaving open the side of the scaffolding that faces the house.

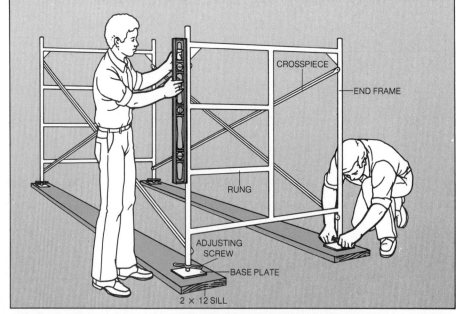

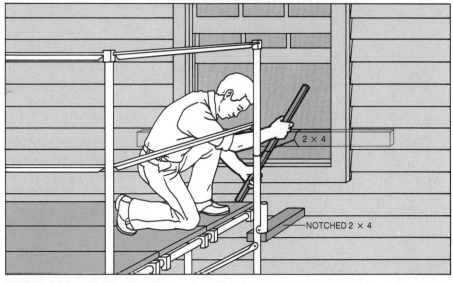

Bracing. When this type of scaffolding is set higher than one story, secure it to the house by notching a 2-by-4 to fit between house and scaffolding, then pulling the scaffolding against this brace with baling wire attached to a 2-by-4 set across the jambs inside a window. If no window is convenient, fasten the wire with a 20-penny nail driven into a stud; in a masonry wall use a lag bolt and a shield in a mortar joint.

Anatomy of a shed dormer. The skeleton of a shed dormer consists of three walls and a roof bearing on four long plates. The front wall consists of corner posts and conventional window framing set in studs that may be unevenly spaced to avoid floor joists and house rafters; this wall stands upon the top plate of the house wall. The dormer side walls are 2-by-4s notched to fit around rafters above, thus providing nailing surfaces inside as well as out. They rest on 2-by-4 plates nailed through the roof to doubled rafters.

The dormer rafters, usually made of the same size lumber as the house rafters and positioned directly above them, bear on a plywood ridge plate that is nailed to the doubled side rafters as well as to the new cut ends of the rafters that are partly cut out when the old house roof is removed. Within the skeleton of the dormer, the dormer ceiling joists tie the dormer front wall to the house rafters on opposite sides of the ridge.

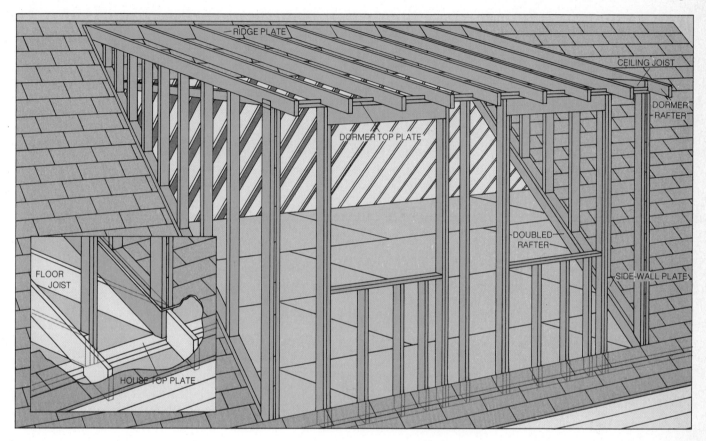

Building the New Front Wall

1 Doubling the side rafters. To reinforce the rafter on each side of the planned dormer, nail to it a board of the same dimensions, duplicating the end cuts that fit ridge and plate with the aid of a T bevel. Use tenpenny nails spaced 6 inches apart in a zigzag. Also butt-nail through the ridge beam into the end of the reinforcing pieces.

Near the ridge and again near the plate, drill small holes through the sheathing and shingles along the dormer side of each doubled rafter.

2 Outlining the dormer. Straddle the ridge and, with a helper standing on a ladder, use the holes you drilled in Step 1 as guides to snap chalk lines above the dormer-side edges of the doubled rafters. Between these two lines, snap a third, parallel to the eaves and 2 feet up the roof from the planned location of the dormer front wall.

4 Probing for the top plate. For a dormer whose front wall rests over the house wall, saw toward the eaves along one of the chalk lines that marks double rafters, starting at the cut made in Step 3 and stopping when you estimate that the blade is near the top plate of the house wall. Probe through the saw cut with a stiff wire while a helper inside the attic watches to tell you how much farther you must cut to reach the plate. Saw a little farther and probe again, repeating this process until the cut is directly above the outside edge of the plate. Make a similar cut at the other side of the dormer, then snap a chalk line between the ends of the two cuts.

For a dormer with a front wall set behind the house wall, mark the line at the planned location of the dormer front wall.

3 Cutting through the roof. Working from a 2-by-10 platform set on roof jacks that you have slipped under shingles and nailed to the sheathing (*inset*), cut along the chalk line that runs parallel to the eaves. Set the blade of a circular saw to the combined thickness of shingles and sheathing—find this dimension from the holes drilled in Step 1—and cut only as far as the chalk lines between the eaves and the ridges. Remove the roof-jack platform.

5 **Prying up a section of roof.** After cutting through the roof along the new chalk line, saw into manageable pieces the rectangle of shingles and sheathing within the four cuts you have made. Then, working from the scaffolding, pry off and discard the sections of roof.

6 **Setting the corner post.** Build two corner posts (*page 46*) with ½-inch spacers; make them long enough to reach within 3 inches of the planned ceiling and cut one end of each to match the slope of the roof (*page 56*). Cut away shingles (*inset*) with a utility knife so that each post can be set on the sheathing above the doubled rafter.

Plumb the post right to left and toenail it front and back through the sheathing to the doubled rafter below. About 6 feet up the roof, tack a scrap of 2-inch lumber, nail a brace to it, then have a helper nail the brace to the post when you have plumbed the post front to back. When the corner post is exactly plumb, toenail the sides to the sheathing and to the doubled rafter.

7 **Nailing the dormer top plate.** Working from a higher platform of the scaffolding, nail a 2-by-4 to the tops of the corner posts. If you cannot buy a single straight 2-by-4 long enough to span the posts, splice two straight pieces end to end with scrap nailed across the joint; later support the joint with a wall stud or a header.

If the dormer will not extend from ridge to house wall, shore rafters above and below the dor-mer area; use shoring (page 28) with studs cut to match the roof angle, and toenail shoring to the rafters. Cut the rafters out of the dormer area and, between the doubled rafters, install dou-bled headers of rafter stock (page 26).

JOIST RAFTER

DORMER-TOP PLATE

HEADER HEADER

KING STUD JACK STUD

ROUGH SILL

CRIPPLE STUD

8 **Framing the front wall.** Between the house top plate and the dormer top plate of a dormer that extends to the house wall, install jack and king studs, headers and rough sills for rough win-dow openings (page 46) in the dormer front wall. Nail cripple studs under the sills and full-height studs between window openings. Since all these studs rest on the house top plate, where joist and rafter ends also are located, the studs generally must be located irregularly to avoid joists and rafters, but spacing should not exceed 24 inches.

If the front wall of your dormer is set back from the house wall, nail a sole plate to the attic floor joists at the wall location. Then toenail studs and window framing to both of the wall plates and to the double header installed across the low-er rafters in Step 7.

After framing the front wall, double the top plate. To prevent racking, nail a 1-by-4 as a tempo-rary diagonal bracing running from the top of one corner post to the bottom of the other.

Rafters and Side Walls

1 Aligning a rafter. Lay a spacer of ½-inch plywood about 3 feet long on the shingles above the doubled rafters and 6 inches below the beginning point of the dormer roof. On this spacer set one end of a rafter board 30 inches longer than the dormer roof; lay a ½-inch plywood strip atop the rafter.

As a helper holds the end of the rafter alongside a corner post so the rafter's bottom edge meets the inside corner of the double top plate (*inset*), position the upper end of the rafter so the top of the upper plywood strip is level with the top of the main roof—you may need a second helper. Tack the rafter to the top plate; tack the upper plywood strip to the rafter.

2 Marking for the ridge plate. While your helper steadies the rafter at the corner post, slide the lower plywood spacer up to the upper plywood strip (*inset*). Mark the shingles at the top edge of the lower spacer.

3 Marking the rafter ridge cut. Set a piece of scrap wood on the lower plywood spacer so that the top edge of the scrap meets the top corner of the rafter. Draw along the upper edge of the scrap piece to mark the rafter for the ridge cut, which can be made with the rafter board laid on the scaffolding.

4 Making a ridge plate. Snap a chalk line parallel to the ridge through the mark made in Step 2. Along this line nail into the roof rafters pieces of ½-inch plywood, each as wide as the length of the rafter ridge cut, making a ridge plate reach ½ inch beyond the doubled rafters.

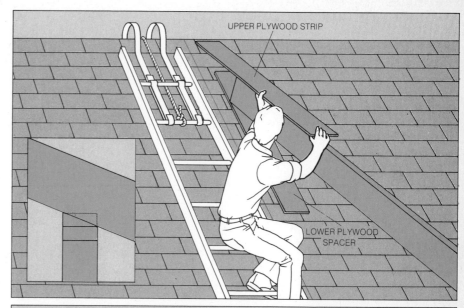

5 **Cutting the bird's-mouths.** Set the ridge end of the rafter on the rafter plate and have a helper hold the rafter against the end of the top plate (*Step 1*) to mark the bird's-mouth cut (*page 58*). Take down the rafter, cut the bird's-mouth, then use this rafter as a template to mark and cut both ends of the other dormer rafters.

Toenail the rafters at 2-foot intervals to the ridge plate, and attach them to the top of the front wall with metal anchors; make sure that the outside rafters are flush with the outside faces of the corner posts and with the ends of the plywood plate. Remove the corner-post bracing installed in Step 6, page 85.

6 **Adding the side-wall plates.** Lengths of 2-by-4 fit on the roof between corner posts and the beginning of the dormer roof to make plates for side-wall studs. Cut the lower ends of the plates at an angle to fit against the corner posts. Using 20-penny nails, face-nail the pieces through the roof into the doubled rafter. Then nail the plates to the corner posts with eightpenny nails.

SIDE-WALL PLATE

7 **Setting the side-wall studs.** Select a 2-by-4 long enough to extend from the house roof beyond the dormer rafters, and set it 16 inches up from a corner post against the inside edge of the side-wall plate. Have a helper hold the 2-by-4 plumb while you mark it at the bottom along the side-wall plate and at the top along both edges of the rafter.

Cut the 2-by-4 bottom along the mark. Then use the marks at the top of the 2-by-4 to cut a notch 1½ inches deep to fit the rafter *(inset)*. Nail the stud to the rafter and the plate, and then, at 16-inch intervals, mark, cut and install studs to fill in both of the dormer side walls.

Completing the Framework

1 **Opening the roof.** For a ridge-to-eaves dormer, level a 2-by-6 laid on the top plate of the dormer wall. Slide the level along the top of the 2-by-6 until it touches the roof, then mark the shingles at this point. Repeat at the other side of the dormer. Connect these points with a chalk line.

Cut away the shingles and sheathing between the new chalk line, the two side-wall plates and the opening near the eaves. For easier handling, cut the roof away in sections between rafters.

2 **Nailing the ceiling joists.** For a ridge-to-eaves dormer, install 2-by-6 ceiling joists between the sheathing on the opposite side of the ridge (*right*) and the outside edge of the dormer top plate (below, shown with a portion of the house roof cut away for clarity). To do so, cut one end of a joist to match the slope of the roof, then cut the other end square to fit flush with the outside of the dormer top plate. Use this joist as a template to cut others. Then, working from ladders on the attic floor, face-nail each ceiling joist to the house rafters on both sides of the ridge with six 16-penny nails. Toenail the ceiling joists to the dormer top plate and face-nail them to the ends of the dormer rafters.

Because dormer end rafters are not set directly above house rafters below, the outermost ceiling joists will not touch dormer rafters at the dormer plate. To fill the gap, add blocking between ceiling joists and dormer end rafters.

For a dormer that does not extend all the way from the ridge to the eaves, the dormer-roof rafters generally serve as joists for a gently sloping ceiling section. Regular ceiling joists are installed between the upper doubled header and the roof rafters opposite the dormer.

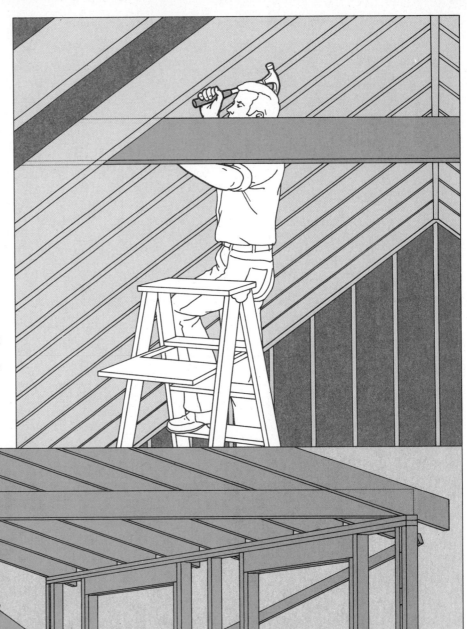

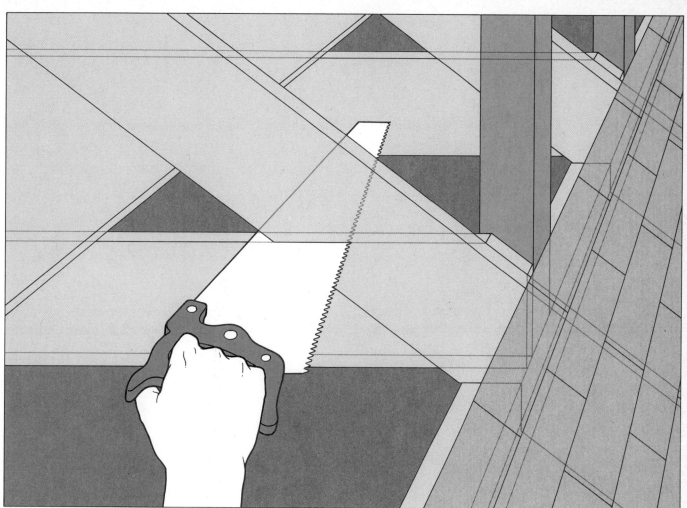

3 **Extracting the old rafters.** For a ridge-to-
eaves dormer, saw through the lower end of each
old rafter within the dormer area, flush with
the old floor joist. You may have to cut vertically
alongside a dormer-wall stud to free the lower
end of the rafter. Then, working from a ladder
while a helper supports the upper end of the
rafter, saw along the bottom edge of the dormer
ceiling joist to free the rafter.

A Miniature House Constructed atop a Garage

If the size of your lot prohibits building outward, or if you want a private studio or an apartment, building above a garage—whether it is attached to the house or freestanding—is a convenient way to expand your home. Garage foundations, built to withstand the weight of automobiles, generally require no further reinforcement to support an added second story. And because your car, and not your family, lives in the garage, you can remove the roof and proceed with construction without disrupting family life. You then have the option of either providing private access to the addition with an indoor or outdoor stairway (pages 100-103, 104-109), or cutting an entryway to connect to the second floor of the house (pages 66-69).

The tricky part of a garage adaptation is the conversion of the ceiling, which was not designed to support activity above, into a floor strong enough for living quarters. If you have a one-car garage—generally no more than 12 feet wide—you need only reinforce or replace the existing ceiling joists before raising the new walls and roof. However, the structural requirements for adding a floor over a two-car garage are more complex.

The size of a two-car garage—usually about 24 feet square—gives a span too great for unsupported floor joists. The problem of providing the necessary support is complicated by the existence of a weak wall in the garage—the wall that contains the garage door or doors. The wide openings make this wall unsound as a bearing wall for the new floor joists.

In a garage with two separate doors, you can install a girder perpendicular to the doors so that the new floor joists are supported by this girder and the side walls; whichever walls supported the old roof can then support the new roof on the addition.

Many two-car garages, however, have only a single, very large door. You cannot install the girder perpendicular to the door, for the girder's end support would obstruct door movement. And unless your garage was originally overbuilt with an unusually heavy steel header over the wide opening, you cannot use the door wall as one of the second-story supports and install the girder parallel to it. In such a case, the best solution is to eliminate the girder entirely and support the second story on truss joists (page 119). They must be at least 14 inches deep, placed on 16-inch centers, and installed parallel to the garage door.

If you have a two-door garage and thus can use a girder, it will be less costly than using truss joists; such a garage conversion is the more common, and it is described on these and the following pages.

Before ordering the girder, prepare the center and end supports for it. The center support should be a 3-inch steel column about 10 inches taller than the distance from garage floor to girder. Order it with a welded-on top plate to hold the girder. It must be set into a concrete footing of the size and depth specified in the local code. To make the footing, you will have to rent a special masonry saw to cut away the floor slab.

The outer ends of the girder can be supported on columns of solid masonry, made by filling cores in block walls or columns; this is the simplest method if you already have masonry walls. If the walls are frame, support the girder ends by putting in steel columns like the center one but precut to a different height —9½ inches shorter than the distance between the foundation and the top of the garage top plate. These end columns will need to have base and top plates welded to them.

For the girder, order a steel beam called a W8-by-18 long enough to reach from one end support to the other. Unless the steel supplier will set a one-piece girder in place for you with a crane, order the girder in two sections predrilled for gussets to connect them together over the center support.

Before you begin construction, diagram all details of your design. If, for instance, you are cutting an entryway through to the second floor of the house, plan to align the floor levels by using joists in the addition the same size as those you find supporting the second floor of the house. If the top plates of the house and garage do not match, plan for a step, with a handrail on each side, between the levels.

When you are ready to begin construction, your first task will be to remove the old roof. If you are building over a two-car garage with overhead doors, you will have to remove them and their overhead hardware temporarily so you can remove ceiling joists or trusses. Work at roof level is dangerous; use the safety accessories and precautions described on page 82.

Much of the material taken from the roof is reusable. Sheathing generally can become a subfloor in the addition; rafters and ridge beams can be recut for joists and studs, and trusses often can simply be taken down whole, then reinstalled to support the new roof.

Removing the Roof

Stripping the shingles and sheathing. Slide a
flat shovel or spade under the roofing to pry up
the roofing nails, and work downward from
each side of the ridge to remove all the shingles.
Next remove the flashing and layers of building paper to expose the sheathing. If your roof is
supported by trusses *(below)*, start
at one end of the roof and pry up just enough
sheathing to free a maximum of three or four
trusses at a time. If you have rafters and a ridge
beam *(page 94, top)*, remove all the sheathing, prying up the sheathing courses that meet at
the ridge before removing the lower courses.

Use a pry bar to remove first the siding and then
the sheathing from the gables.

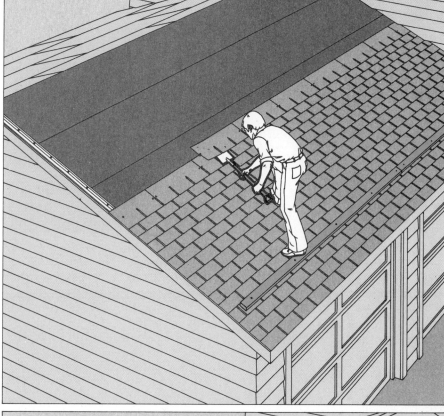

Taking down a truss roof. Remove the end trusses, lower them to helpers on the ground, then
nail diagonal 2-by-4 braces between the exposed
top plates to steady the walls and corners.
Remove the remaining sheathing and trusses in
stages, resting the trusses on top of each other over the diagonal bracing until you are ready to
lower them to the ground.

Removing rafters and ridge beam. Secure a temporary ridge-beam support near each end of the ridge beam (page 59, Step 1)—if the ridge beam is jointed, install an additional support on each side of the joint—and then pry the rafters loose from the ridge beam, ceiling joists and top plates and lower them to the ground. Remove the end rafters and gable studs last. Finally, lift the ridge beam from its temporary supports, and lower it to the ground.

In a one-car garage, you can leave the ceiling joists in place; in a two-car garage, remove them and brace the corners as you would when removing a truss roof (page 93, bottom).

Doubling Joists for Support in a One-Car Garage

Trimming the ceiling joists. After removing the roofing and its supports, saw the ends of the ceiling joists 1½ inches from the exterior edge of the top plates, pulling nails that might interfere with cuts. Cut header joists from the same size stock you will use to reinforce or replace the existing joists, and install them in the space you have cleared along the top plates.

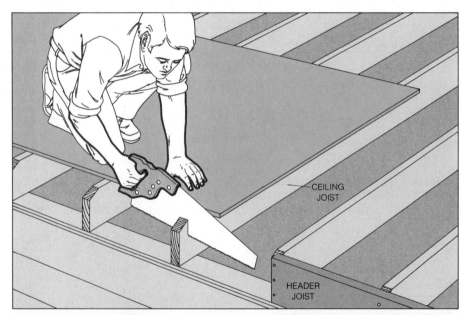

CEILING JOIST

HEADER JOIST

Reinforcing the ceiling joists. If the ceiling joists are larger than 2-by-6s and are set no more than 16 inches apart, you can use them as is. If they are 2-by-6s, strengthen them by doubling. Cut new 2-by-6s to fit between the header joists and position them alongside the old joists; if necessary use wood shims to keep the tops of the new and old joists flush. Nail the new joists to the plates and header joists, and then drive 16-penny nails to secure the old and the new joists to each other at several points along their lengths. If existing joists are more than 16 inches apart, cut additional joists and install them between the doubled ones.

If you are installing larger joists instead of reinforcing the existing ones, use 2-by-8s set on 16-inch centers. The only existing joists you need to remove are those that would conflict with the placement of the new joists.

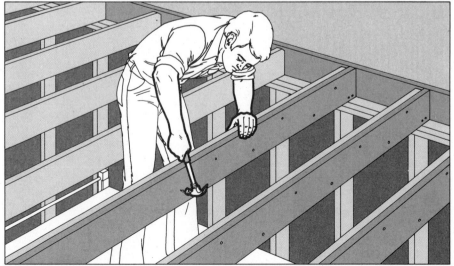

94

Installing a Girder in a Two-Car Garage

1 Providing anchors for the end columns. In the center of the two walls that will support the girder ends, remove wallboard, if any, and a 12-inch section of the sole plate—including the stud if there is one there—to expose the foundation below. Hold each end column in position to outline the two inside base-plate boltholes on the concrete. Then use a carbide-tipped bit to drill ¾-inch holes 4 inches deep at the marks. Drive ¾-inch lead shields into the holes. Secure the cut ends of the sole plate with masonry nails driven down into the concrete slab.

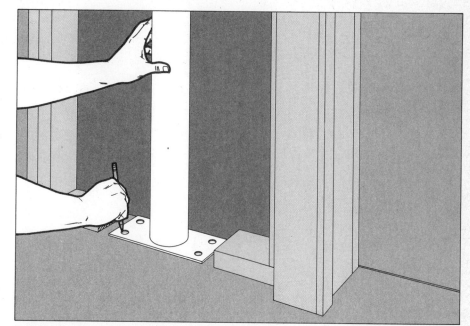

2 Plumbing the end columns. Position a precut end column over the lead shields and start ½-inch lag bolts through the base plate into the lead shields. Nail a scrap of lumber between the studs on either side of the column to hold it within the plane of the wall, and use a level to plumb the column from left to right as you tighten the bolts. If necessary, use slate shims under the corners of the base plate to plumb the column. Repeat for the other end column.

Nail 2-by-4 blocks between each column and the nearest studs, and cut out a 6-inch section of double top plate above each column (*inset*).

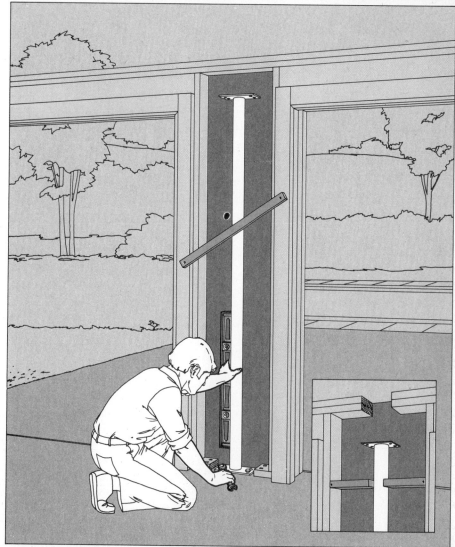

3 **Raising the girder sections.** To provide temporary support for the girder ends that will be spliced together, stack masonry blocks on scaffolding set up 2 feet to each side of the position of the middle column. With a helper for each 3 feet of girder length, raise a girder section into place, first resting one end on the scaffolding and blocks, and then lifting the other end onto its end column. Bolt the top plate of the column loosely to the girder and then level the girder section with slate or steel shims under the other end before tightening the bolts. Position and level the second girder section in the same way and bolt both sections together with predrilled steel splice plates (*inset*). Check the level along the top of both girder sections.

If you have ordered a single long girder, have professionals set it in place over the end columns. Level it along the top by wedging temporary 4-by-4 or doubled 2-by-4 supports beneath it.

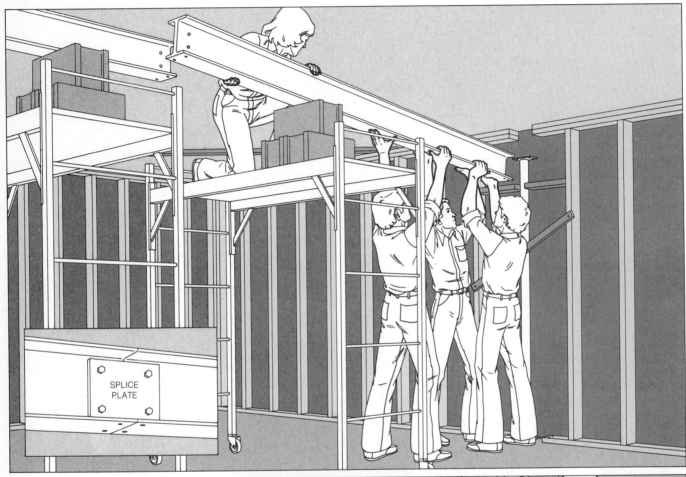

SPLICE PLATE

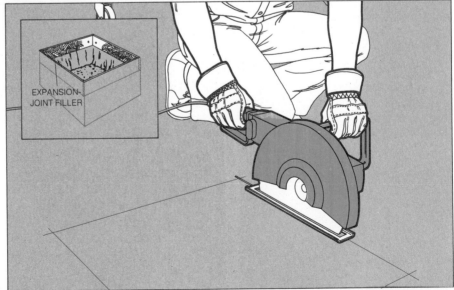

EXPANSION-JOINT FILLER

4 **Digging a footing for the center column.** In the center of the garage floor, and in line with the two end-column positions, mark off a square for the footing size required by your local building code. Wearing goggles, face mask and gloves, use a rented masonry saw to cut through the concrete slab along the marks. Remove all the concrete within the cuts you have made—use a sledge hammer and cold chisel to break it into chunks if necessary—and dig a hole to the depth required by the code. With masonry nails, attach expansion-joint material along the edges of the slab inside the footing hole (*inset*).

5 Setting the middle column. Bolt the top plate of the middle column loosely to the girder through the predrilled holes and let the base of the column hang down into the footing hole. Shim the column plumb with bits of slate while a helper tightens the bolts. Then fill the footing hole with concrete level to the existing floor. Allow the footing to set for 3 days before removing the scaffolding and proceeding with the job.

Fitting a Girder into a Masonry Wall

1 Chiseling out girder pockets. Wearing goggles and gloves, chisel a 10-inch section from the top course in the center of the walls that will support the girder ends. Tamp mortar down into the cores of the blocks below the girder pockets; if possible, fill the cores down to the footing.

If one of the walls to receive a girder end is a common wall between the garage and house, you must remove a section of block from the middle of the wall, level with the opposite girder pocket. A section of guttering can serve as a funnel when you pour mortar to fill the blocks below.

2 Installing bearing plates. Spread a ½-inch bed of mortar on the bottom of each girder pocket and tap a 6-inch square of ¼-inch steel plate into the mortar, leveling it with a torpedo level. Directly above each bearing plate, cut out a 6-inch section of top plate.

When the mortar below the girder pocket has cured, lift the girder sections into place *(page 96)* and level them. The top of the girder should be 1½ inches below the surface of the top plate; if the height of the girder needs adjusting, use additional bearing plates—available in several thicknesses—to shim the girder ends. Finally, splice the girder sections together and set the middle column.

The Upstairs Floor and Walls

1 Securing a plate over the girder. Attach 2-by-6s to the top of the girder, cutting them to reach the exterior edges of the top wall plates they intersect, and fastening them with bent-over 16-penny nails. Drive nails two thirds of the way into the edges of the 2-by-6s at 12-inch intervals and bend the protruding nails around the top flange of the girder. Nail a length of metal strapping atop the intersections between girder and wall plates to secure the joints (inset).

Install a joist plate (page 58) along the common wall of the house and garage to support the floor joists that will be installed there.

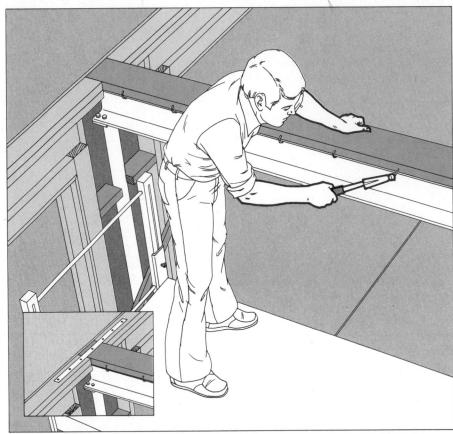

2 Laying out floor joists. Starting 15¼ inches from one wall, mark lines on 16-inch centers on the joist plate of the common wall and on the top plate of the opposite wall. Stretch a chalk line between pairs of marks on the two walls, holding it at the bottom of the joist plate and at the top of the top plate, then snap it to mark the girder. Install the remaining header and the stringer joists (page 40), and then place floor joists on the one side of the marks along the plate and on the opposite side along the common-wall joist plate, so that the joists overlap on the girder.

Secure the joists with joist hangers at the common-wall header, toenail them to the top plate and header of the opposite wall, toenail them to the girder plate, and nail the overlapping joist sections to each other.

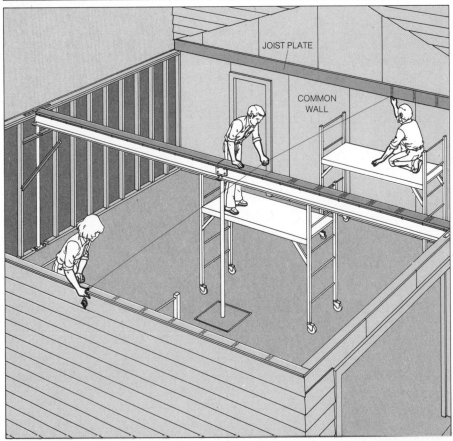

JOIST PLATE

COMMON WALL

3 **Installing the subfloor.** When laying a plywood subfloor over offset joists, plan so that a break between rows—in this case between the third and fourth rows—falls over the area where the joists overlap. If necessary, cut the plywood sheets to fit. Lay the plywood lengthwise across joists, centering end joints over a joist; stagger end joints, and install nailer blocks between joists beneath the side joints of adjacent rows. After the break over the overlapping joists, repeat this pattern.

Haul materials up to the finished subfloor and use it as a work platform to frame sections of the second-story walls (*pages 42-47*).

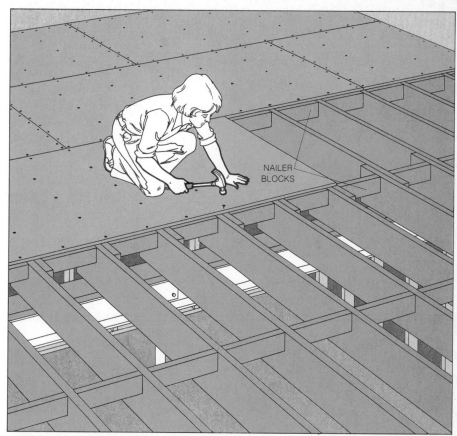

NAILER BLOCKS

4 **Raising the second-floor walls.** Raise each framed wall section into place against vertical stops nailed to the header or stringer joists, tilting it up with 2-by-4s hinged by one nail to the middle and end studs. Plumb and level the wall section, and then brace it in place by nailing the free end of each 2-by-4 used for tilting to a 2-by-4 block nailed to the subfloor. Follow the procedures on pages 42-47 to secure the wall sections to one another and to the existing house.

STOPS

A Fire-resistant Indoor Stair

The easiest way of providing access to a second-story addition above an attached garage is to cut a doorway in the second story of the main house—but it is not the only way. If you want privacy for a studio or apartment in the addition, or if an entry directly from the main house would lead through a bedroom, you may prefer to build a new stair, rising either inside the garage, as described in these pages, or outside *(pages 104-109).*

An interior stair is protected from the weather; it is comparatively flexible—the steps can lead down either to an exterior door or directly into the first floor—and it is easy to build. However, fire hazards in a garage require safety features not otherwise needed. The stairway must be separated from the garage by walls sheathed with fire-resistant wallboard of the type called 1-hour rated. And if the stairway opens at the bottom into the garage, this opening must be fitted with a solid-core wooden door 1¾ inches thick.

The simplest stair well to build runs parallel to the upstairs floor joists—and in most garage additions, these joists run parallel to the front and back walls. Thus the only simple location for inside stairs is along the back wall with the entire stairway run to one side of the central supporting girder, as shown here. If you must run the stairs along a side wall, perpendicular to the second-story joists, you can do so by framing these joists as you would for a bay window *(pages 24-26).*

Wherever you place the stair, you must meet standard safety requirements: a minimum horizontal clearance of 2½ feet between a top or bottom step and a door; at least one handrail 30 inches above the front edges—called the nosings—of the treads; equal step heights, called unit-rise heights, between 6 and 8¼ inches; equal tread widths of at least 9 inches; and headroom clearance between treads and the open end of the stair well of at least 6 feet, 8 inches.

Start planning the stair's dimensions by measuring its total rise—the distance from the garage floor to the upstairs finish floor. Divide the rise in inches by 7, and round off to the nearest whole number to determine the number of risers. Then divide the total rise by the number of risers to get the exact unit rise.

To determine the unit run—the tread depth less the overhang of the nosing—use this formula: the unit rise plus the unit run should equal 17 to 18 inches. For example, if the unit rise is 7½ inches, the unit run can be 9½ to 10½ inches. To set the exact unit run, choose a figure halfway between the two—in this example, 10 inches. Though the treads will come from the lumberyard already shaped with nosings, which should overhang the risers by ½ to 1⅛ inches, use the unit-run figure when you mark and cut the 2-by-12 boards, called carriages, that support the treads and risers.

To find the stair's total horizontal distance, or total run, multiply the unit run by the number of steps. The length of the stair-well opening usually equals the total run, so the opening extends over the bottom stair; you can shorten the well to gain floor space upstairs, but you must keep 6 feet, 8 inches of headroom between the edge of the well and the stairs.

1 Preparing for the stair-well opening. For a stairway at the rear of a garage parallel to upstairs floor joists—the simplest to build—use the methods shown on pages 95-97, Steps 1-5, to erect a girder; then install floor joists, but omit joists over the area to be occupied by the stairwell. Install a triple joist between the girder and the side-wall top plate, locating this joist as far from the garage rear wall as the width of the well, usually 3 to 3½ feet.

2 Framing the stair-well opening. Install double headers between the triple joist and the rear-wall stringer joist, then attach short joists, called tail joists, between the double headers and the side walls. Fasten the triple joist and tail joists to the headers with joist hangers; fasten the stringer joist to the headers with right-angle framing connectors. Finally, double the stringer joist between the headers.

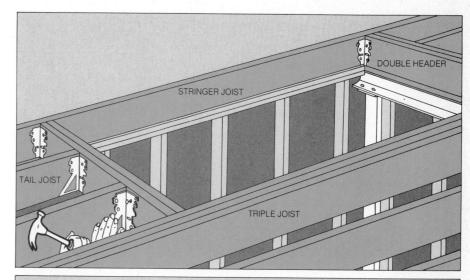

3 Marking the bottom end of the carriage. Set a framing square near one end of a 2-by-12 that is at least 12 inches longer than the length of the stair—the diagonal distance along the stairway from upstairs floor or to downstairs floor. Place the unit-rise and unit-run figures on the outside scales of the square touching the upper edge of the board (in this example, the figures used are 8 and 9½ inches); then mark the outline of the square's outer edges (right, top). Extend the unit-run line to the lower edge of the board and, to its right, mark a parallel line at a distance equal to the thickness of a tread (right, bottom). The second line represents the cut for the bottom of the carriage, the end that will rest on the floor.

Move the framing square to the right so that the unit-run figure touches the end of the first unit-rise line, then set the unit-rise figure at the upper edge of the board and, once again, mark the outline of the square. Moving along the board, repeat this procedure until you have marked one more pair of unit runs and rises than the number of steps calculated for the stair.

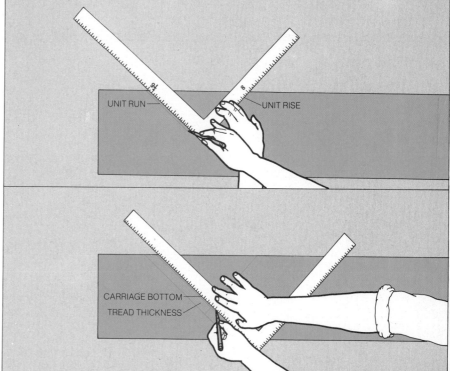

4 Marking the top end of the carriage. Extend the top unit-rise line to the lower edge of the carriage. Cut along both this line and the top unit-run line to fit the carriage to the header of the opening in the upstairs floor.

Cut along the bottom end line marked in Step 2, then cut along the unit-rise and unit-run lines. Use the carriage you have cut as a template for cutting two additional carriages.

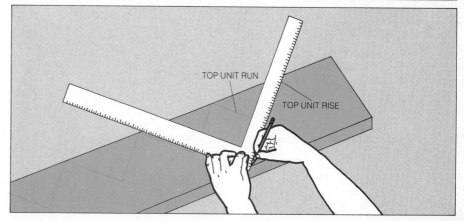

5 Installing the carriages. After checking that the unit-run cuts are level, secure the carriages to the header with framing connectors, using one connector on each of the outside carriages, two on the middle carriage. Nail the carriage that rises along the garage wall to the wall studs.

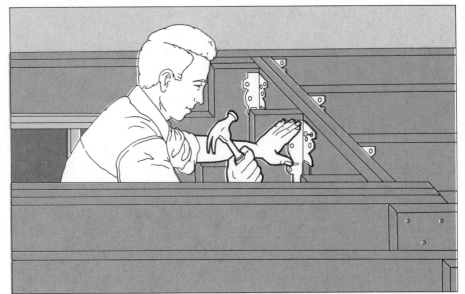

6 Installing spacers. Cut four 2-by-4 spacers to fit between adjoining carriages. About a third of the way up the stair, toenail one end of a spacer flush with the top of a unit rise in the carriage at the garage wall, then face-nail through the middle carriage into the other end of the spacer. Nail a second spacer between the middle and outside carriages, and install the second pair of spacers two thirds of the way up the stair.

7 Putting in treads and risers. Cut risers from 1-by-8s or 1-by-10s and secure them to the riser cuts with finishing nails, then cut treads to the overhang you have chosen, and nail them. Under the carriages, nail through the faces of the risers into the edges of the treads.

8 **Installing a sole plate for the stair well.** Cut a 2-by-2 to fit between the sole plate of the side wall and the lower edge of the outside carriage at the floor. Toenail one of the ends of the 2-by-2 to the sole plate; face-nail the last 6 inches of the other end to the carriage.

9 **Framing the downstairs wall.** Beginning at the header cut of the outside carriage, cut 2-by-3s to fit at 16-inch intervals between the lower edge of the carriage and the bottom of the triple joist of the stair-well opening. Face-nail the lower ends of the 2-by-3s to the carriage and toenail their tops to the joist; add 2-by-2 blocking to the carriage between these studs as nailing surfaces for wallboard. Between the end of the carriage and the door wall, nail full-height 2-by-3 studs to the sole plate and to the joist.

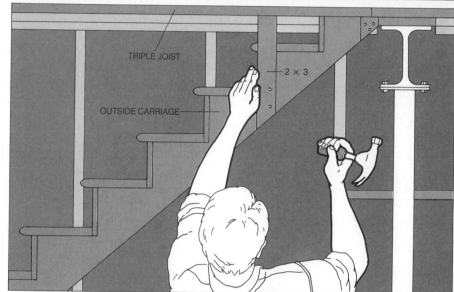

TRIPLE JOIST

2 × 3

OUTSIDE CARRIAGE

10 **Framing upstairs walls.** On the upper floor, frame conventional stud walls at the long side and the enclosed short side of the well opening; at the head of the stairs, frame a third wall with a rough opening for the upstairs door. If you need a new exit door downstairs, frame it in the garage wall at the end of the first-floor landing.

Use fire-resistant wallboard to sheathe stair and landing walls downstairs, the bottom of the carriages, and the garage ceiling; upstairs, standard wallboard is acceptable on walls around the stair well. Attach a handrail 30 inches above step level, screwing rail brackets to studs.

When Space Is Precious: Outdoor Stairs

An outdoor stairway provides a private entrance for a second-story addition and does so at no sacrifice of interior space. For a small addition built over a garage, it may be an indispensable spacesaver.

Protect the stairway from rotting and warping by using pressure-treated wood and by coating cut ends with a commercial wood preservative. Concrete piers and a concrete base—either a floating slab about 4 inches thick if codes permit or a slab with its footing below the frost line *(right, top)*—will protect the wood from ground moisture and termites. Build the stairway with galvanized fasteners and paint it with an oil-base deck paint. For the treads, mix 1 part of fine-grain sand to 8 parts of the paint to create a slightly gritty, nonslip finish.

Before ordering the wood, you must know the exact dimensions of the stairway. Start your planning by marking off the landing, or platform, beneath the second-story door. On the addition wall mark a point 5 inches below the threshold and 4 inches outside the doorjamb opposite the head of the stairs; on the other side of the door, mark the wall 5½ feet from this point to locate the stair end of the landing. The height of the points above the ground, less 2 inches (to allow for the height of the concrete base), is the total vertical rise of the stairway; use the method on page 100 to calculate the total horizontal run, and drive a stake at the bottom of the stair.

If the siding of the ground floor is set in slanted courses, use shims to make vertical nailing surfaces for the platform and the inner carriage. Shim clapboard siding with pieces of clapboard turned upside down; to shim other angled sidings, such as shakes or shingles, use cedar shakes. To install the platform and its support posts, you will need a scaffold. The simple scaffold shown here consists of ordinary planking, metal braces and pump jacks (available at rental agencies), and two 10-foot uprights. Nail 2-by-4s face-to-face to make the uprights, driving the nails into both sides of an upright at 1-foot intervals.

Anatomy of an outdoor stair. This typical stairway is supported by three 2-by-12 carriages; the innermost carriage is bolted to the studs of a garage wall, and all three are secured to a platform landing. In some areas the carriage bottoms can rest on a 4-inch-thick concrete slab without fasteners; in the example shown here, to meet code requirements, the base extends below the frost line and each carriage is secured to it. The inner edge of the platform is bolted to the second-floor header joist; the outer edge rests on 4-by-4 posts, which rest on concrete piers. Planks for the treads and the platform floor are ¼ inch apart for drainage. On the balustrade, guardrails are nailed to the posts; cap rails protect the end grain on each post.

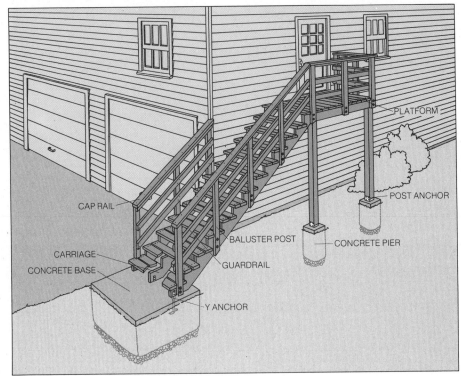

CAP RAIL

PLATFORM

POST ANCHOR

CARRIAGE

CONCRETE BASE

BALUSTER POST

CONCRETE PIER

GUARDRAIL

Y ANCHOR

BRACE

BOLT

A Scaffold Raised by Jacks

1 Raising the uprights. Bolt and nail each brace near the top of an upright, with the bolt of a brace crossing the seam of an upright; then set the uprights 10 feet apart and 32 inches from the wall, with the long arm on each brace running toward the doorway. (In very soft ground, set the uprights in holes 4 inches deep.) Fasten the braces to the wall with nails driven through the siding and into the second-floor header joist.

2 **Operating the scaffold.** Attach a pump jack to each upright, lay 2-by-10 planks across the jacks to form a platform and, with the aid of a helper, raise the scaffold by pumping the foot levers on both jacks at once. To lower the scaf- fold, depress the stationary rod at the base of the jack and turn the crank *(inset)*. If you must raise or lower the scaffold without a helper, do not move one end up or down more than a foot before bringing the other end to the same level.

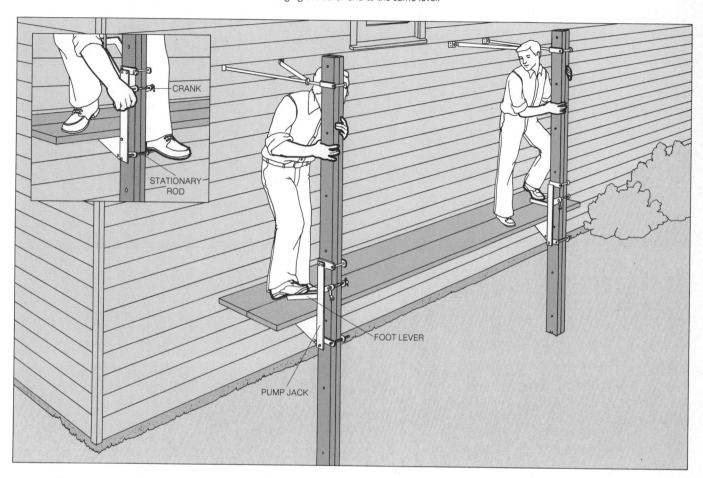

Building the Stairs

1 **Assembling the platform frame.** Working on the ground, butt-nail four 2-by-8s together to form a frame 66 inches long and 36 inches wide. Within the frame, nail a 2-by-8 joist parallel to the long sides and centered between them.

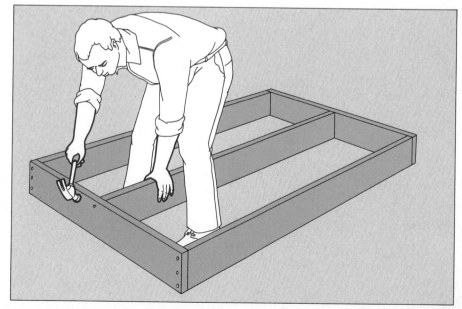

2 **Installing filler strips.** Nail three shims to the wall below the doorway to provide bolting surfaces for the ends and the middle of the platform frame and, while a helper holds the frame against the shims, mark the gaps between shims on the edge of the frame. Nail filler strips of 1-by-4 scrap to the side of the frame, between the marks and flush with the top of the frame.

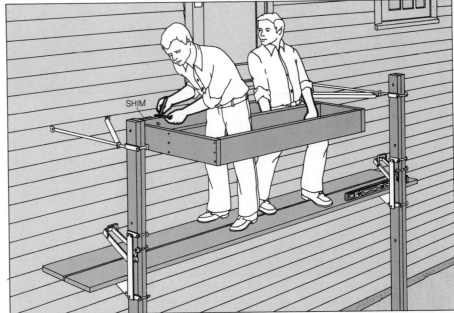

SHIM

3 **Securing the platform frame.** Fasten the frame in place with 4½-inch lag bolts driven through the shims and into the second-floor header joist and have a helper hold the frame level. Set two temporary 2-by-4 braces on the ground and nail them to the outer face of the frame. Caulk the joint between the frame and the wall.

Drive pairs of nails into the top of the frame 4 inches from each outer corner, tie a string between each pair of nails and hang a plumb bob from the center of each string (inset).

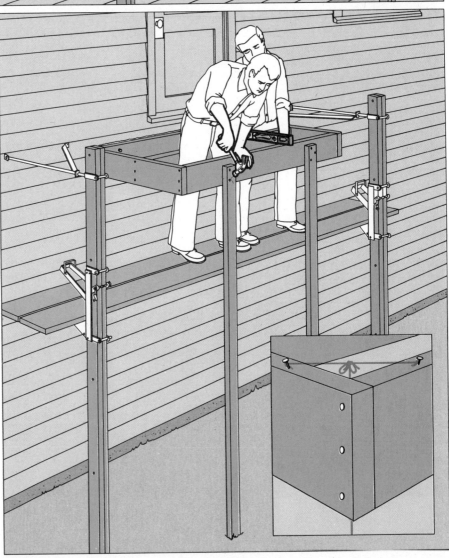

4 Digging holes for the footings. Dig holes for the piers beneath the platform, using the plumb bobs to mark their centers. Those holes should extend below the frost line—your building department can tell you the required depth. Fit the mouth of each hole with an 8-inch-square form made of 2-by-4s held in place with stakes; set a 2-by-4 as a bridge between the forms and use a level on the 2-by-4 to set the tops of the forms at the same height.

Prepare a corresponding hole and form, 4 feet square, for the stair base. If the frost line is very shallow in your locality, or if your local code permits a floating slab in this situation, dig the hole 4 inches deep; otherwise, dig it to the same depth as the pier holes, as shown below. In either case, locate the hole so that the last step, at the position marked by a stake (*text, page 104*), will rest fully on concrete and the greater portion of the base will lie in front of this step.

5 Setting the post and carriage anchors. Spread a 2-inch layer of gravel in each hole, pour the concrete and set 8-inch anchor bolts (*page 39, Step 7*) for the piers.

If you pour a floating slab for the base, you can simply rest the carriages on it; if the base extends deeper than 1 foot (*right*), fit it with anchors by the following method. After pouring the concrete, bend three Y-shaped framing anchors so that the wings are 1½ inches apart, and push an anchor into the concrete at each point where a carriage will rest. To brace the anchors as the concrete hardens, run a wire through all six wings and twist the wire ends around nails driven partway into the sides of the form.

After the concrete has dried take final measurements for the stairway and cut the carriages (*page 101*) and the 4-by-4 platform-support posts.

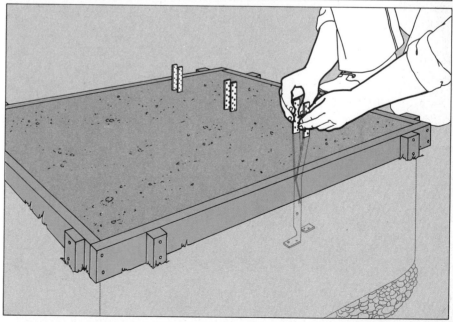

6 **Attaching the post anchors.** On each pier, slide the base of the post anchor down over the anchor bolt, add the offset washer and screw the nut on loosely—you may need to adjust the base and washer to plumb the support post later. Set the post support inside the base.

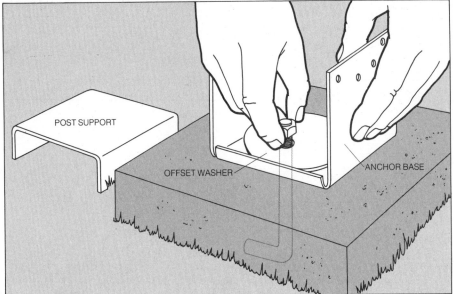

POST SUPPORT

OFFSET WASHER   ANCHOR BASE

7 **Installing the support posts.** Nail the support posts inside the outer corners of the platform frame, set each post on a post support and, while a helper holds the post plumb, adjust the position of the post anchor and tighten the nut. Nail the flanges of the anchor to the post. Remove the scaffold and the temporary braces.

With a helper, hold a carriage of the stairway in position against the wall and, using the bottom edge as a guide, scribe a line along the wall. Shim the wall at each stud location to make a vertical surface for bolting the carriage in place.

8 **Securing the carriages.** Rest the bottom of the inner carriage on the concrete base and attach the top of the carriage to the platform frame with a right-angle framing connector *(page 101, Step 2)*; bolt the carriage to the wall through the shims and, if the base has anchors, nail their wings to the carriage. Attach the other carriages at top and bottom and install spacers between the carriages *(page 102, Step 6)*.

Cut a 2-by-4 baluster post, 45 inches long, for every third stair that will be protected by a handrail. Miter both ends of each of these posts to match the angle of the carriage bottom. The bottom posts that will rest on the concrete base need be mitered only at the top, the post for the top step need be mitered only at the bottom. Cut four unmitered posts for the platform.

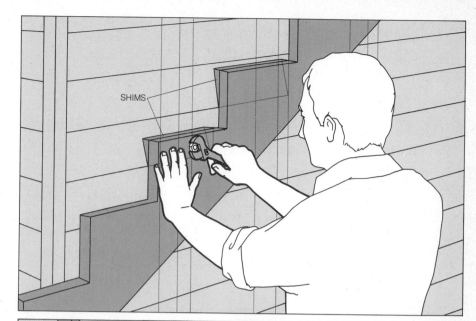

9 **Installing the baluster posts.** Using two lag bolts in each post, bolt each baluster post to the outer carriage and to the freestanding part of the inner carriage at the position of every third stair. On the platform frame, bolt the unmitered posts at the two corners opposite the top stair and at the centers of the two outer sides.

Cut two 2-by-6s, 38 inches long, for each tread; notch the ends as necessary to fit around baluster posts *(inset)* and, working from the bottom up, nail them to the carriages with ¼ inch of space between them and a 1½-inch overhang. Cut 2-by-6s, 38 inches long, as platform flooring boards and nail them to the frame, using the same notching and spacing.

10 **Putting on the rails.** Nail three 2-by-4 guardrails to the insides of the baluster posts, mitering the ends where the stair rails meet the platform rails. Cut a 2-by-6 cap rail, mitering the ends for the joints at the head of the stair and at the outer corner of the platform, and nail this rail to the edge of the upper guardrail. If you must join sections of cap rail, make the joint between baluster posts: the exposed end grain of each post must be completely covered.

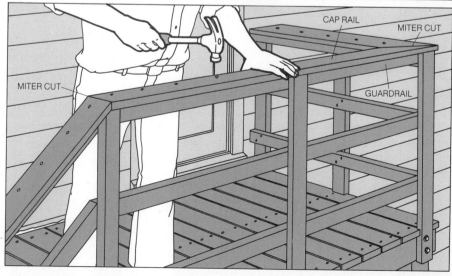

4 The Major Addition: A New Wing

Some people would rather move than build a major addition—commonly a collection of rooms that becomes a separate wing. Indeed, moving is preferable in economic terms if by combining the money you would spend on an addition with the proceeds from the sale of your house, you can buy a different house better suited to your needs. But there are other factors to consider when deciding whether to expand your house or sell it and move on to another. If your present home is in a convenient location, if your family has strong ties to the community, or if you are just plain attached to the house, even an extensive and expensive addition may be an attractive alternative to a new house.

Moreover, some types of additions will increase the market value of your house—some, but not all, and not on every house or in every neighborhood. If property values in your area are decreasing, it could be financially unwise to add space to your house. And, if your house is so large or luxurious that it is already the envy of your neighbors, to add a major improvement would be overbuilding. Still, an addition may well be worth more than its cost. In particular, if you own a house that by comparison to its neighbors is small or outmoded, a lavish and well-planned addition can be a profitable undertaking. A good guiding principle is that the best house to expand is one that will become the second best on the block when you finish.

Some kinds of additions increase value more than others. A new or enlarged kitchen, extra bedrooms, or a large family room can add as much as 100 per cent of their cost to the value of the house (extra baths generally add more than their cost) if you do most of the building yourself. On the other hand, you might want to think twice about adding bedrooms to a house that already has four, or a family room to a house equipped with a den. Most buyers have no need for that amount of duplication. Be conservative with finishing touches. Luxurious bathroom fixtures rarely return the extra money they cost, and even a fireplace, though a selling point, will not repay its cost if you must also add a new brick chimney.

These pros and cons of marketplace economics must be considered carefully, particularly when undertaking a major addition to a house, but they rarely dictate what people finally decide to do. Nor should they. Your residence, after all, is not a piece of business property that should be expected to produce a dollars-and-cents profit. It is a place for you and your family to live comfortably and enjoyably. Comfort and enjoyment are the most important measures that go into the bottom line of the accounting for an addition; if the improvement seems worthwhile to you personally, its potential future value to someone else is secondary.

Extra Steps for a Major Addition

The job of erecting a major addition seems forbidding at first glance, but the appearance is deceiving. Though the components of the addition—foundation, walls and roof—are larger than those described in Chapters 2 and 3, they demand no new skills and surprisingly few additional techniques.

Foundations of large additions, for example, commonly require additional underpinning to support wide expanses of floors (pages 115-117). But the masonry of the underpinning is no more difficult than that needed to build a foundation for a small addition. Exterior walls may be so long that they must be raised in sections and spliced together, but the splices are matters of simple carpentry. Interior partition walls, neither necessary nor desirable in most small additions, are almost always built into large additions, and they must be spliced to the exterior walls (pages 118-119).

Building the second story of a two-story addition is no different from raising walls atop an existing garage (page 99). For wide additions, the ceiling joists and rafters used in small additions can be replaced with prefabricated, easily installed roof trusses (pages 126-129). All of the finishing touches—roofing, siding and weatherproofing on the exterior, flooring and wallboard on the interior—are installed by conventional methods.

The basic services and utilities are another matter. Though you can found, frame and roof a large addition with the same techniques used for small ones, heating it, cooling it and supplying it with electricity may require a degree of expertise that is not called for in a small structure. The chances are that the furnace or air conditioner in your house does not have the capacity to heat or cool the addition. You may choose to replace your old system with a larger unit that can serve new pipes or ducts running into the addition. Or you may choose to install separate heating and cooling plants for the addition alone.

For electricity, it is likely that you will need a subpanel in the addition, wired to the main service panel in the house. From this unit you can run branch circuits through the addition as shown on pages 70 through 75. Depending on your experience with furnaces, air conditioners and wiring, you may decide to hire out some of these jobs to professionals.

You probably will want a bathroom in a larger addition. Putting in the new pipes presents no unusual problems for the initiated home plumber (pages 120-125), unless it involves tapping into an existing drain line that is more than a vertical distance, specified by your local code, away from plumbing fixtures. In that case hiring a plumber may speed the work—and, in the case of a new drain connection, may be a legal necessity.

Anatomy of a two-story addition. In the crawl space of this addition to the back of a two-story house, concrete-block piers support the central section of a wooden girder, fitted at both ends into pockets in the foundation walls, and the inner ends of the first-floor joists rest upon the girder. On the first floor, directly above the girder, a bearing wall supports the joists of the second floor. A doorway in this wall, as in any bearing wall, would have to be framed with an especially strong header (page 47).

Roof trusses, which bear entirely on the outside walls of the addition, require no bearing wall above the girder, but any interior walls built into the second story must be fastened to the trusses to keep the walls from wobbling.

ROOF
TRUSSES

PARTITION
WALL

JOISTS

HEADER

BEARING
WALL

GIRDER

PIERS

JOISTS

Supports to Beef Up Foundation and Frame

The difference between the foundation and frame walls for a large addition and those for a small one *(Chapter 2)* lies in details. They are important details. Some are simple to handle but others may best be left to a professional.

If the addition will have plumbing directly connected to the sewer, for example, most local codes require the connection to be made by a licensed plumber. If you have to hire him for that part of the job, it makes sense to have him complete rough installation of the drains—before you pour footings. In slab construction, water pipes and heating pipes or ducts that come through the slab, as well as drain pipes, must be stubbed out before the slab is poured, a job most easily handled by professionals.

Most other work for a large addition is fairly simple, although some of it may be time consuming. Steps for an exterior door require a slab to rest on, for example; you have to dig a trench to match the dimensions of the steps and pour the footing for the addition and the slab at the same time.

To support 2-by-10 floor joists of an addition on a block foundation wider than 15 feet, you need a girder of wood or steel; if you are using 2-by-12 floor joists, they can span 18 feet without a supporting girder. A wooden girder is less expensive than steel and a little lighter, but a steel girder can be less work if fewer piers are necessary than for a wooden one. Get girder dimensions and pier spacing from your local building code. The pier illustrated is made of standard masonry blocks—available everywhere—but the job goes faster if you use such alternate materials as 12-inch square hollow blocks or corrugated-cardboard forms for poured-concrete piers.

A slab foundation usually requires no extra reinforcement to support the floor, regardless of dimensions, so long as you are building a one-story addition. But to support the second-story floor in a two-story structure, you must either use truss joists *(page 119)* or provide a bearing wall in the first floor. In an addition with a crawl space, this wall would rest on a steel or wooden girder. But a slab should be reinforced with a concrete "girder," called a grade beam, to support the weight of the floor above.

A Girder Parallel to the House

1 **Making girder pockets.** As you build the foundation walls, lay solid blocks at every location where a girder will rest, following the pattern indicated in bold outline. In the top course make a girder pocket with one or two solid partition blocks—half as thick as a standard block—set flush with the outside of the wall.

2 **Placing piers.** Build piers to support the girder, spacing them as required by the building code.
For each pier, dig a footing hole 2 feet square
in line with the girder pockets. Make the holes the
same depth as the foundation footing unless
you will use a girder of 2-by-12s. In that case, dig
holes 1½ inches deeper. In each hole make an
X of steel reinforcing bars supported on bricks,
and tie to it vertical bars at opposite corners.

Pour an 8-inch footing, then lay the piers,
grouting the blocks as you go. In the top course of
a pier for a wooden girder, set 12-inch metal
anchor straps in the grout. No anchor straps are
required for a steel beam.

REINFORCING BARS

BRICK

3 **Building a wooden girder.** Construct the girder
inside the foundation walls. Using lumber of
the width specified by code for the span, cut two
boards 1 inch shorter than the distance between the outsides of the wall pockets and fasten
them with 16-penny nails every 10 inches in
a zigzag pattern. If the girder spans more than
16 feet, splice boards, staggering joints so that
they will rest on the piers.

4 Notching the sill plate. If you are using a wooden girder, enlist a helper for every 5 feet of length, place the girder on the sill plate and then mark and cut a notch for the girder in the plate. If the girder is made of 2-by-12s, cut a notch 1½ by 4 inches in each end (*inset*); otherwise no notch is needed. Set the girder in place and shim at pockets and piers to level the girder flush with the sill plate. Nail the girder to the anchor straps in the piers.

If you are using a steel girder, you will require one helper for every 3 feet of girder to lift it. Use steel shims to level the girder so that it lies 1½ inches below the sill plate, then fasten a plate to the girder as shown on page 98, Step 1.

A Girder at Right Angles to the House

1 Installing the girder. One end of the girder goes into a hole in the house foundation; the other end fits into a girder pocket (*page 114*). To make the hole in the house foundation, remove a section of block below the sill plate; the section should be 16 inches wide and 1 inch shorter than the height of a wooden girder, or ½ inch taller than a steel girder. Fill the blocks below the hole with concrete to make a level surface. Build a wooden girder (*page 115*) or order a steel one to fit flush with the inside of the wall. In the end of the wooden girder, cut a 1½-by-8-inch notch so that the girder fits under the sill plate, install the girder and shim it flush with the sill. Shim a steel girder so the plate (*page 97, Step 2*) is flush with the sill.

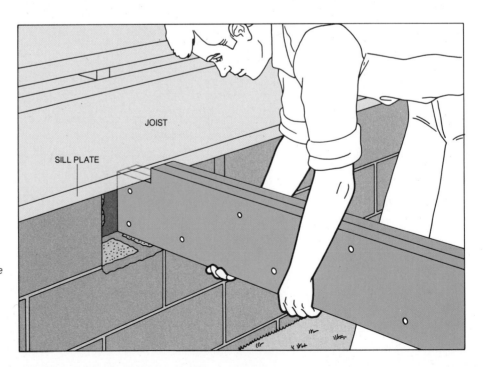

2 **Bricking up the foundation.** Fill in around a wooden girder, leaving a ½-inch air space at the sides to prevent moisture from collecting. Trim bricks about 1 inch shorter than the spaces on both sides of the girder, then mortar the bricks in place. For a steel girder, no air space is needed; fill extra space with mortar.

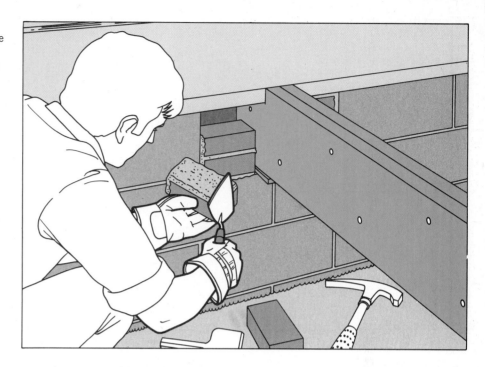

A Grade Beam for a Slab Foundation

A concrete rib in a slab. When you dig footings for a slab *(page 41)* that will support an interior bearing wall, dig a trench 8 inches wide and 8 inches deep where the wall will be constructed. In the trench, lay four lengths of ½-inch reinforcing bar, supported and separated from one another by bricks. Tie the reinforcing bars in the grade-beam trench to those in the perimeter trench, then pour the slab.

Framing Tricks for the Big Addition

Although the studs and plates of a long wall are assembled much like those of a short one *(pages 45-46),* a few special techniques are called for in a large addition. For ecomomy and safety in handling, no part of a wall should exceed a length of 16 feet; longer walls are generally assembled in sections, and the sections must be tied together to form a sturdy wall. A doubled top plate, which ties corners together in small additions, also ties wall sections together in large ones. The upper top plates *(right, top)* are nailed to the main plates of each section and span joints by at least 4 feet on each side.

When an interior partition is used to divide the big interior space of a large addition, an assembly of special studs is built into the frame for support; the partition is nailed to the assembly and the subfloor, then tied to the exterior wall of the addition with a double top plate fitted into that of the wall *(opposite, top).*

Tying wall sections together. Wherever two sections of the new wall meet, double the top plates of the sections with a length of 2-by-4 that overlaps each section by at least 4 feet. Complete this double plate, making the upper part of the plate bridge the joints of the lower by at least 4 feet on either side. If the two parts of the plate do not align precisely, force them into line by toenailing at an angle through the side of the upper part and into the top of the lower.

Securing a Partition Wall

1 Making the nailing assemblies. To prepare a nailing surface for each end of the partition, cut three 2-by-4s to stud length and assemble them in a U-shaped trough, with the sides of the U nailed to the bottom. When you construct the exterior walls of the addition, butt-nail these nailing assemblies to the top and sole plates of the wall at the points you have chosen for the partition, with the bottom of the Us flush with the inside edges of the plates.

2 **Nailing the partition in place.** Assemble the partition wall in the conventional way *(pages 45-46)* and raise it into position, then nail its sole plate to the subfloor and its outermost studs to the nailing assemblies in the exterior walls.

To secure the partition to the top plates of the exterior wall, cut out the parts of these plates that lie directly above the nailing assemblies, and double the partition top plate with a 2-by-4 that fits into the cutout notches and extends the full length of the partition *(inset)*.

An Unconventional Joist

A two-story addition often occupies a space so wide that no single conventional floor joist can span it. The usual solution to the problem is a pair of joists supported at the center by an internal bearing wall or by a girder *(pages 95-98)*. But there is an unusual solution, too—a so-called truss joist, consisting of two strips of laminated wood, one above another, joined by a sheet of plywood or an open mesh of metal webbing. Truss joists are expensive and must be made to order by a fabricator, but they are strong enough to span large distances without intermediate support and they enable you to create large uninterrupted spaces or to place partitions wherever you please.

For spans greater than 18 feet—the longest distance a 2-by-12 joist can safely bridge—the truss joists commonly used in residential construction

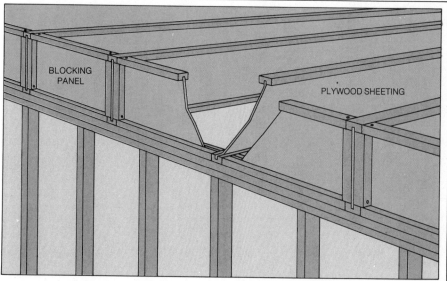

are made with sheets of ⅜- or ½-inch plywood. The joists are mounted at 24-inch intervals and toenailed to the top plates of the exterior wall. To stabilize them, blocking panels are provided, to be set between the ends of joists and toenailed to the plates and top joists.

Truss joists are available from building suppliers nationwide; allow at least three weeks for delivery.

Tapping the House Pipes for New Plumbing

For anyone with a working knowledge of standard materials and techniques, installing plumbing in an addition can be a straightforward job, easily divided into manageable stages if, as is frequently the case, the new supply pipes and drainpipes can conveniently be run into the existing plumbing system.

In a ground-floor addition, the work is simplest if your house has a basement with a cinder-block foundation wall and you provide a crawl space for the addition. More complex are installations involving either a house or an addition built on a slab (drains would then have to run below the concrete) or the need to make holes in a poured-concrete foundation wall, which can be weakened by the process of breaking through; in such cases, you may want professional help.

However, in the common case of the cinder-block basement linked to a crawl-space addition, you can easily run pipes through the foundation wall and build in framing to support fixtures. In a second-story addition, new fixtures can be placed above existing ones, and pipes can be connected directly to the original plumbing lines.

To make such jobs easier, take advantage of the opportunity to install pipes at an early stage of construction. Locate the exact positions of the new fixtures and install the underfloor pipes before you sheathe the floor, while there is still light and room in the uncovered crawl space.

New plumbing in a ground-floor addition should be plotted from the main drain in the addition (the drain of a toilet in a bathroom or powder room, of a sink in a kitchen or wet bar) to the main stack of the house. The new lateral drain line must drop ¼ inch per foot; if a long run of pitched drainpipe would be an obstruction in a finished basement, you can build a partition to house the pipe, or you can use elbows to route the pipe along the basement walls.

Pipes and fittings made of plastic are lightweight, inexpensive and easily marked; use them wherever your local code allows, and use the smallest permissible pipes. For example, 3-inch pipe is standard for the main vent stack in most areas, but many codes permit a new second stack to be reduced to 2-inch pipe above the highest toilet drain. A reducer fitting, cemented onto the new stack just above the toilet-drain connection, switches the stack to 2-inch pipe.

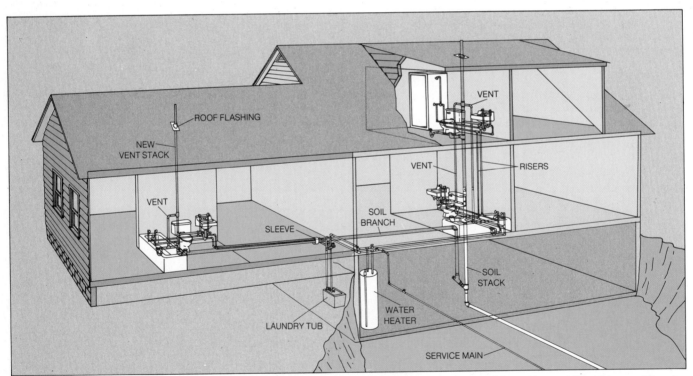

Old plumbing and new. Though no single house and addition would match this drawing exactly, the plan shows how to link the original main-house plumbing to new plumbing for additions. The original plumbing (*white*) serves a kitchen, a laundry tub and a bathroom. (For clarity, kitchen plumbing and the laundry-tub drain are not shown.) Supply pipes carry hot and cold water to the fixtures. All fixtures drain into a soil stack, in which wastes move by gravity to the sewer. Above the fixtures, the stack functions as a vent, letting air into the system.

To this existing system are linked new bathrooms (*gray*) in a ground-floor addition and a shed dormer. From the new downstairs bathroom a drain branch runs through a sleeve in the common wall to the main stack. New supply lines, tapped from old ones at the point nearest the addition, also run through the sleeve.

For the shed dormer, a new line vents the downstairs lavatory drain and connects to a stack extension upstairs. The original bathtub vent is disconnected and runs up to the extended stack. Supply for the upstairs bathroom is through risers—vertical extensions of ¾-inch supply pipes.

Adapting the Framing for Pipes and Fixtures

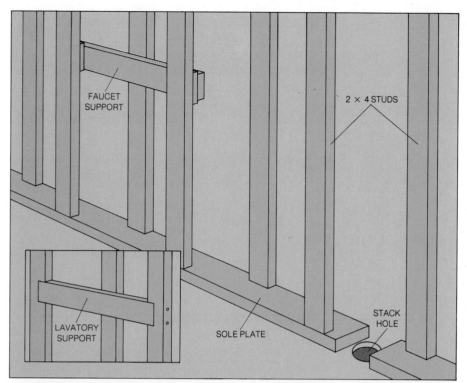

A wet wall. An extra-thick wall, with 2-by-6s for the sole plate, top plate and end studs, accommodates a 3- or 4-inch soil stack; the stack hole is set into a gap in the plates. Horizontal runs of supply pipes and drainpipes will run between staggered 2-by-4 studs, set along the edges of the plates so that a stud occurs on an opposite edge every 12 inches.

Supports for tub faucets and shower heads are nailed to 2-by-4 studs at the positions called for in the manufacturer's rough-in specifications. To support a lavatory (*inset*) set a 2-by-4 crosspiece, 24 inches long, against two studs, with a 1½-inch overlap on each side. Mark the outline of the overlaps at the height indicated by the rough-in specifications, notch the studs to fit the crosspiece flush with the front of the studs, and nail the crosspiece in place.

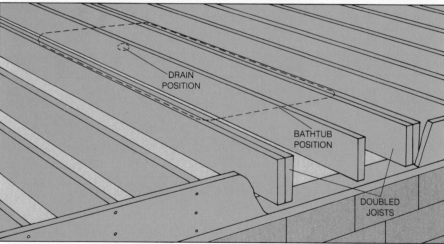

Supports for a tub. Doubled joists bear the heavy weight of a tub filled with water. Between the doubled joists, the single joist directly beneath the tub is offset by a few inches to allow room for the drainpipe of the tub.

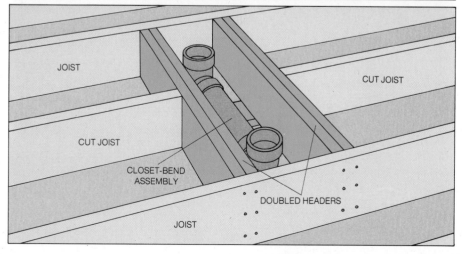

A cut joist for a closet bend. To make room for a toilet closet-bend assembly that lies across the floor joists, a gap is cut in the intervening joist, and the cut joist is reinforced with doubled headers. The four header pieces are nailed to both the uncut joists and the ends of the cut joist. The closet-bend assembly is supported from below by a crosspiece nailed between the headers.

Putting In a Branch Drain

1 A route to the foundation wall. Locate and mark the point at which you will break through the common foundation wall by the following method. Determine the location of the main fixture drain in the plumbing—in this example, the closet-bend assembly of a toilet. Test-fit the assembly with an elbow for a horizontal drain line and, using scrap wood or cinder block, support the assembly temporarily at its planned location, with the end of the elbow at least an inch below the joists. Measure the horizontal distance from drain end to the foundation wall, allow ¼ inch of vertical drop for each foot of horizontal run, and mark the wall for a 9-inch hole.

With a hammer and chisel knock out blocks to make a passage at the mark. Fit the hole with a short sleeve of 8-inch cast-iron or steel pipe.

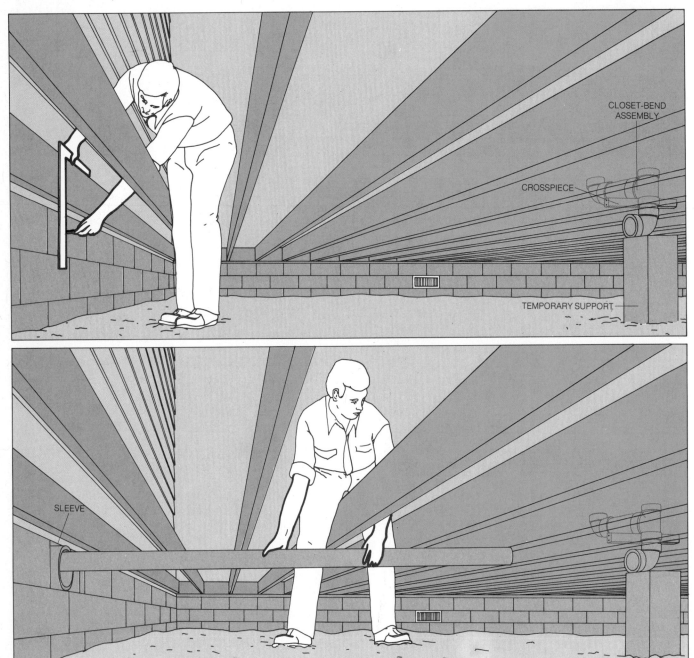

CLOSET-BEND ASSEMBLY

CROSSPIECE

TEMPORARY SUPPORT

SLEEVE

2 Running the drainpipe into the addition. Have a helper in the basement of the main house slide a 4-inch drainpipe through the sleeve and into the crawl space of the addition. Test-fit the pipe into the elbow on the closet-bend assembly and suspend the pipe from the joists with metal straps nailed to the joist at 4-foot intervals. Hang one side of each of the straps temporarily on a finishing nail to permit later adjustment of the slope of the drainpipe.

3 Adjusting the pitch. Extend the drainpipe to the soil stack in the main house and, starting at the closet-bend assembly, adjust its pitch by changing the loops of the straps. To set the pitch, use a level with a strip of wood taped to one end to make the level read true at a pitch of ¼ inch per foot—for a level 2 feet long, use a strip ½ inch thick; for a 4-foot level, a 1-inch strip. (For clarity, existing drains have been omitted.)

4 Connecting the pipe to the soil stack. Unscrew the cleanout plug in the main stack and use a threaded plastic adapter to join a plastic Y to the cleanout fitting. Fit a quarter bend onto the drainpipe and test-fit a vertical run of pipe into the Y—be sure that you do not alter the slope of the branch line. Cement a test cap to the bottom end of this pipe, and a new cleanout fitting to the diagonal branch of the Y.

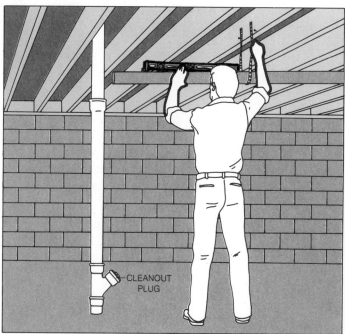

CLEANOUT PLUG

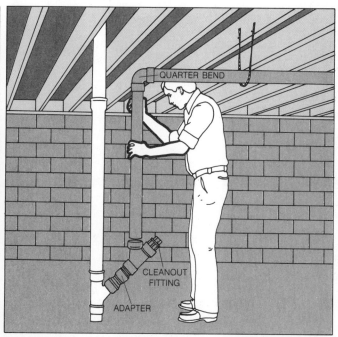

QUARTER BEND

CLEANOUT FITTING

ADAPTER

5 Setting the sleeve. At the hole in the foundation wall, lay a bed of mortar beneath the sleeve to set it in a position that allows a ½-inch clearance beneath the drainpipe. Fill the rest of the hole around the sleeve with mortar and brick chips. Recheck the slope of the drain, and secure the metal straps permanently with common nails.

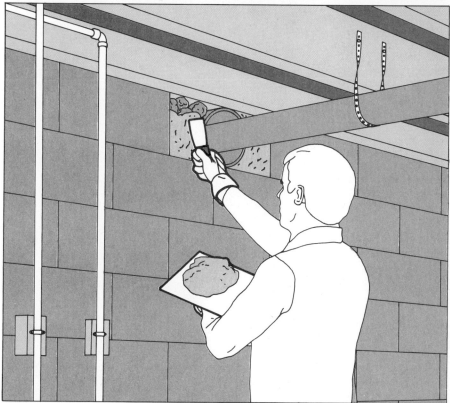

Running Supply Pipes

Tapping the lines. Though the supply-pipe routing shown here may not match the layout of your own house, you can use the method of its construction in any pipe route. Shut off the water supply in the main house and drain the runs of ¾-inch hot- and cold-water pipes that are closest to the sleeve in the foundation wall. Cut out sections of the hot- and cold-water pipes and install T fittings angled for direct routes to the sleeve. Install stop-and-waste valves for the new lines, run the pipes to the sleeve, keeping them parallel and at least 4 inches apart, then run the pipes through the sleeve and extend them into the crawl space on opposite sides of the drain branch.

Insulating the pipes. In the unheated crawl space beneath the addition, slip lengths of tube-like rubber insulation over the supply pipes. Secure the insulated pipes to the joists with pipe hooks, slanting the pipes slightly so that they will drain back into the main house. Pack loose insulation into the sleeve around the pipes and cover the drainpipes and the underfloor fixture traps with standard blanket insulation. Before proceeding to the final stage of the job (below), install risers to raise supply pipes above the floor; complete the new subfloor, framing and sheathing, and install horizontal piping to bring all the new plumbing to the rough-in point.

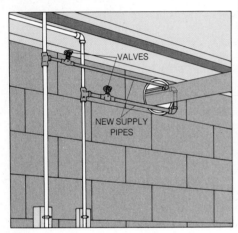

VALVES

NEW SUPPLY PIPES

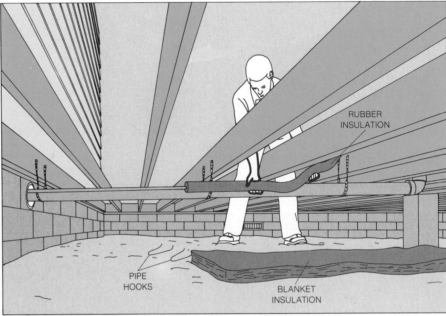

RUBBER INSULATION

PIPE HOOKS

BLANKET INSULATION

Venting the New Drain

Raising the stack. To locate the point where the vent stack will pass through the top plate of the wet wall, drop a plumb line from the plate to the center of the stack. Mark the position of the string and cut a hole slightly larger than the vent pipe through the top plate and into the attic. Use the same method to determine where the stack will pass through the roof and cut a corresponding hole in the roof. If your local code permits a 2-inch vent stack in this installation, cement a 3-by-2 pipe reducer into the sanitary T on the closet-bend assembly and use 2-inch pipe to extend the stack through the roof.

LAVATORY LOCATION

REDUCER

SUPPLY PIPES

Simple Upstairs Plumbing

1 Cutting the old vent stack. At the location of the new second-story plumbing—in this example, a bathroom in a shed dormer, have a helper hold the existing vent stack firmly in place while you sever it with a pipe cutter. Make the cut near the floor of the addition—the more pipe you removed upstairs, in an open work area, the less you will have to remove downstairs, where fixtures in the existing bathroom will cramp your work space. After the cut is made, have your helper hold the cut pipe in place on the stack until you can join him to lift it off and remove it.

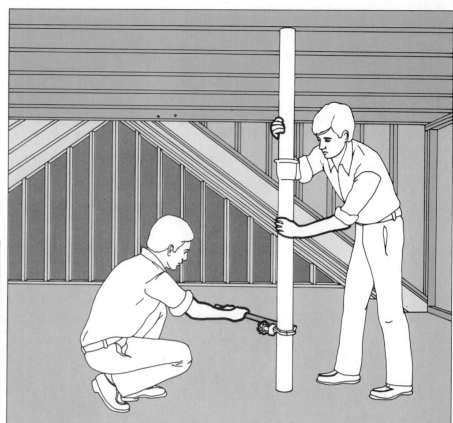

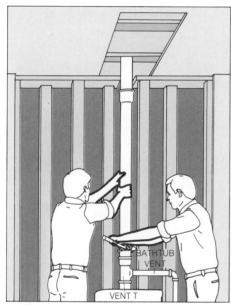

BATHTUB VENT

VENT T

2 Opening the pipes downstairs. Remove enough wallboard to expose vents in the downstairs bathroom, and enough of the ceiling to install the new closet-bend assembly. Protect the fixtures with drop cloths and cut the stack about 3 inches above the vent T. With a helper remove the upper section of the stack. Stuff a rag into the stack to catch debris, use a chisel to break out the pipe remaining in the hub of the vent T, then clear out the rag and debris. Install a plastic adapter at the T and fit a length of plastic stack pipe to reach the level of a new closet-bend assembly upstairs.

Remove the horizontal section of existing vent pipe from the T and close the opening at the side of the T with a pipe plug. Remove the elbow on the vent line and fit a plastic adapter onto the vertical section of the old vent. If, as shown here, the lavatory drain is not vented separately, install a T in the drain about 2 feet from the stack and fit the T with a plastic adapter. Connect new plastic vent lines to the adapters and extend these lines to a level at least 6 inches above the upstairs lavatory.

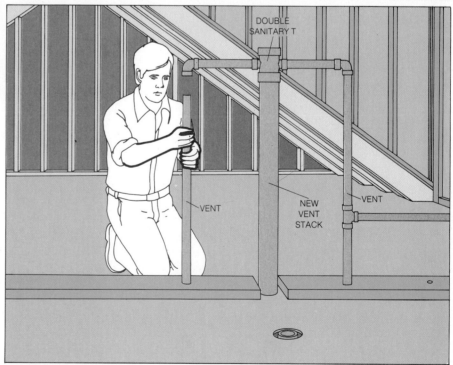

DOUBLE SANITARY T

VENT

NEW VENT STACK

VENT

3 Reconnecting the vents. Secure the sole plate of a wet wall on the upstairs floor and install the drain and vent lines for the upstairs fixtures in the usual way. To vent the downstairs fixtures, install a double sanitary T in the vent stack 6 inches or more above the overflow level of the upstairs lavatory, and connect vertical extensions of the old vent lines to the stack. Finally, extend the vent stack upward to the height above the roof required by your building code.

A Network of Trusses for a Wide Roof Span

To roof an addition more than 18 feet wide, use prefabricated trusses, which eliminate the need for interior bearing walls. Trusses can be used for virtually any style of roof, from the simple gable shown here to a hipped roof that fits together like a jigsaw puzzle.

On an addition that does not have interior partitions, trusses are erected just as they are on a freestanding structure. If the addition roof is to run into a side of the house, simply nail the last truss to the house wall *(page 59)*. If the ridge of the addition roof will run into the house roof, as shown on these and the following pages, the new roof is mated to the old with a ridge beam and jack rafters.

As you carry each truss inside the addition, lift its ends onto the top plates of the walls and tilt it upright in a single, simple operation.

On an addition with partitions *(page 130)*, the interior walls make it impossible to carry the trusses inside: you must slide the trusses up an outside wall (or pay a crane operator to lift them for you) and stack them flat atop the addition, then tilt them upright as you normally would.

Order the trusses three to five weeks before you will need them. Give the truss supplier a set of working drawings for the addition, complete with precise figures for the slope of the addition roof, the heel height *(page 57, center)* of the house roof, the width of the addition including sheathing, and the length of the addition (less the house overhang, if any). If the slope of the addition roof must match that of the house roof, many truss suppliers will measure the old roof themselves; others will ask you for the measurements described below.

Measuring to match a slope. Inside the attic or overhead crawl space, measure the distance from the top of the existing ridge beam to the bottom of a joist or, if you have a truss roof, the distance from the point of a truss to the bottom of a bottom crosspiece. Then measure across the attic between the outside edges of the top plates on which trusses or joists rest.

RIDGE BEAM

JOIST

Raising the Trusses

1 **Positioning anchors.** Starting 2 feet from the far end of the addition, fasten framing anchors every 2 feet along the top plate of each side wall. For the truss that will be nearest the house, place the anchors so that the truss will rest in front of the house fascia board.

FASCIA

FRAMING ANCHOR

2 **Securing a nailer.** Using a 2-by-4 as a spacer, nail 2-by-4s to the top plate of the addition end wall 1½ inches back from the outside edge of the plate. Make sure that nailer ends are flush with the outside edges of the side top plates.

3 **Bracing for the end truss.** Nail two 10-foot 2-by-4 stops through the sheathing into the studs that divide the end wall into thirds. Position the stops so that they project 6 feet above the top plate, and nail them to the top plate and the studs with at least four 16-penny nails.

Working on the ground, sheathe the gable-end truss. Cover the ventilator framing installed by the manufacturer, then cut an opening in the sheathing to accommodate the ventilator.

4 **Erecting the end truss.** With two helpers, lift the ends of the truss, apex down, onto the top plates of the side walls, then roll the truss upright, using a 2-by-4 to push the apex of the truss until the top chords rest against the stops.

Shift the truss if necessary to make the overhangs the same on both sides of the addition, then nail the top chords of the truss to the stops and the bottom chord to the nailer. Use a long 2-by-4 fastened to the ventilator framing to force the truss plumb, then nail the brace to a 2-by-4 stake pounded into the ground.

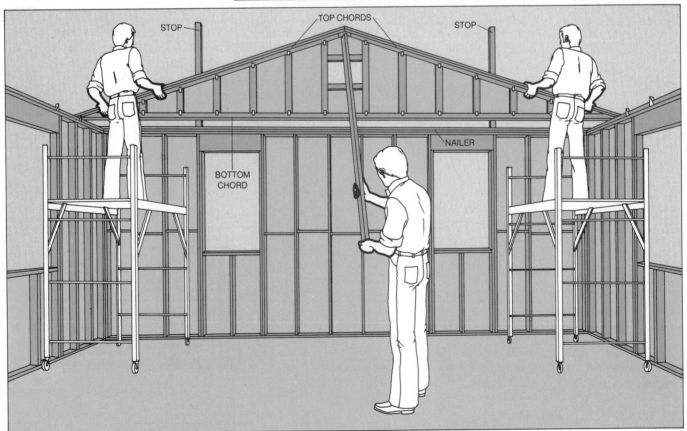

STOP   TOP CHORDS   STOP

NAILER

BOTTOM CHORD

5 **Laying out the overhang.** Stretch a string between nails on the end of the end truss and the
house fascia board to align overhangs. Place
the fascia nail a distance from the addition wall
equal to the overhang of the end truss.

Erect the truss next to the end truss using the
techniques described in Step 4. Align the
overhang with the string guide and nail the bottom chord to the framing anchors.

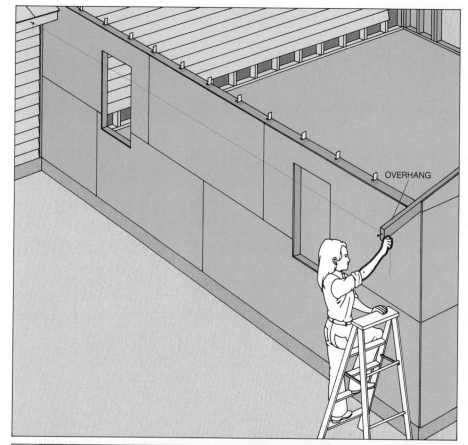

OVERHANG

6 **Aligning the trusses.** Nail the end of a 1-by-6
to the middle of a top chord; measure 2 feet along
the board and mark the position of the second
truss. Have a helper hold this truss at the mark
while you nail the 1-by-6 to the truss and install a second 1-by-6 temporary brace on the opposite side of the roof.

Erect, anchor and brace all but the last four
trusses in the same way as the second. Roll all the
last four onto the addition wall at one time and
lean them temporarily against the house while you
anchor and brace the trusses one at a time.

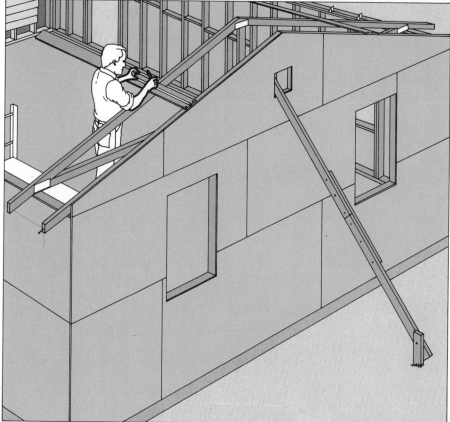

Trusses over Interior Walls

Putting up the trusses. Mark the positions of the trusses on the side-wall top plates, but do not install framing anchors at this stage of the job. Lift the trusses over the gable-end wall and stack them horizontally in threes on top of the walls and partitions. Tilt the truss nearest the house up-right, plumb and brace it to the house temporarily with a 2-by-4 nailed to the house roof, then fasten the truss to the top plates with framing anchors *(below)*. Erect the other trusses in the usual way *(page 129, Steps 5 and 6)*, working out from the house to the end of the addition.

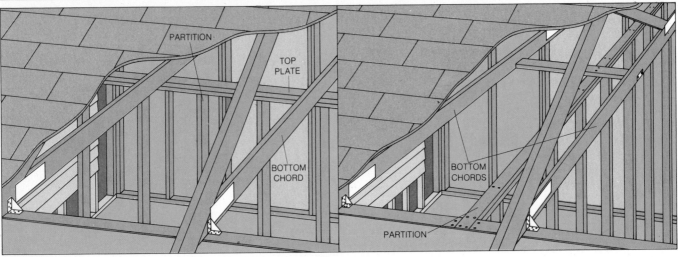

Securing the interior partitions. After the roofing has been applied and the bottoms of the trusses have settled, fasten the bottom chords of the trusses to the top plates of the partitions. Where a partition runs perpendicular to the trusses *(left)*, toenail the bottom chords of every second truss to the top plate of the partition. Where a partition runs parallel to the trusses and between two of them, butt-nail a 2-by-4 block between the bottom chords of the trusses every 4 feet and nail through the block into the top plate of the partition *(right)*.

Fitting a Truss Roof to a Main Roof

1 Marking ridge-beam cuts. Mark the center line of the addition up the existing roof with a chalk line, then, while a helper holds one end of a long 2-by-4 on edge on top of the truss nearest the house, move the other end up and down the center line to level the 2-by-4. Next, set a scrap of lumber on the roof, against the 2-by-4, to mark it for a diagonal cut *(inset)*. Then cut the 2-by-4 to make a ridge beam extending from the truss peak to the existing roof.

2 Securing the ridge beam. Butt-nail the 2-by-4 to the truss so that the top edges of the ridge beam meet the top edges of the top chords of the truss. Secure the other end of the ridge beam by nailing through the house roof and into a rafter, or into a block between rafters. Then nail a 2-by-4 across the top chords of the truss and under the ridge beam to support it *(inset)*.

Attach 2-by-4 extensions to the top chords *(inset)* of the truss nearest the house to help install roof plates and jack rafters as described on pages 60-61, Steps 3 through 7. After installing the rafters, remove the 2-by-4 extensions and sheathe the roof, detaching the 1-by-6 braces on the top chords of the trusses as you go along. Then use the 1-by-6s to connect permanently the bottom chords of the trusses.

A Professional Second-Story Job

With the help of a few friends, a skilled homeowner can build almost any addition—from a bay window to a two-story wing—beautifully and economically. But in practice, some additions persuade all but the bravest to hire professionals. One such project is a full second story on a one-story house.

Most additions are structurally independent of the houses they expand, but a second story depends on the walls below to support it. Moreover, the first-floor layout of the house generally must be radically altered to accommodate the second story. To make these alterations successfully, the builder must find the right answers to difficult questions: if there is no interior bearing wall in the house, what will support the new floor? Where will the new staircase fit?

While such structural complexities can be circumvented with shrewd adaptation of standard techniques, a major practical obstacle remains: to install the new, higher roof for a full second story, it generally is necessary to remove the old roof first, exposing the house to weather. The family cannot live in the house while the work goes on.

Even roof removal may be avoided, of course, if the existing house has a flat or nearly flat roof, more common in the Southwest than elsewhere in the United States and Canada. In such a case, the old roof can be left in place permanently, and second-story flooring, walls and roof may be built on top of it. Such a grafting operation, was performed for the unique, elaborate addition diagramed on the opposite page. The family lived in the main house during the construction, which took professional builders six months to complete.

The owners wanted additional bedrooms away from the children's rooms. They also wanted to enlarge their foyer, expand their kitchen and convert a bedroom into a family room. These changes added 1,000 square feet to their 1,800-square-foot home.

The new second floor runs the length of the front of the house and occupies slightly more than a third of the depth, using an off-center bearing wall to support the back of the addition.

The first task that faced the builder was to cut openings in the bearing wall to accommodate the enlarged foyer and the new family room. The old roof and its covering were left undisturbed except in two areas, where they were removed to accommodate the staircase and to create a cathedral "ceiling" in the family room. The second-story floor joists rest on doubled 2-by-4 plates that were nailed through the existing roofing to the first-story bearing walls.

After a spring and summer of construction and disruption, the addition was ready to live in. It worked perfectly, especially in isolating the children from the parents. Because of the air space between the ceiling of the first story and the floor of the second, the grown-ups in the master suite upstairs never hear youngsters in the bedrooms below.

A layer-cake house. The one-story house at bottom left was transformed into the two-story house below by the structural changes shown in the drawing on the opposite page. In the drawing, three layers of the house—the original ground floor, the new support framing for the addition, and the addition itself—are separated to show the method of construction.

Alterations in the ground floor not only accommodate the addition, but also use existing space more efficiently, generally by removing walls (*broken lines*). To create space for a new staircase and to enlarge the foyer, one wall was removed from the left front bedroom, and a small room next to the guest bath was taken out entirely. The wall separating the kitchen from the right front bedroom was removed to make a large family area.

After these alterations were made, the contractor built the layer of support framing directly onto the nearly flat roof of the original house. The staircase, which has no bearing wall for support, is framed by doubled 2-by-10 joists. Floor joists are set in a huge rectangle of framing members, supported at the front and near the back by long, doubled plates. Over the carport and the front entrance of the house, the support framing rests on steel columns.

The new second floor, secure on this bed of framing, has a master-bedroom suite and a guest room. To keep the house from looking like a box on a box, end walls of the addition were given a slight pitch; inside the addition, these pitched walls create a large storage area at one end of the house and the cathedral "ceiling" of the family room at the other.

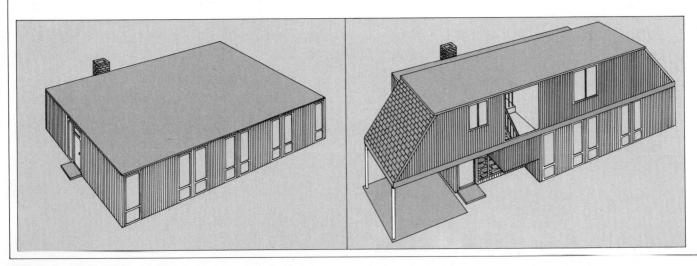

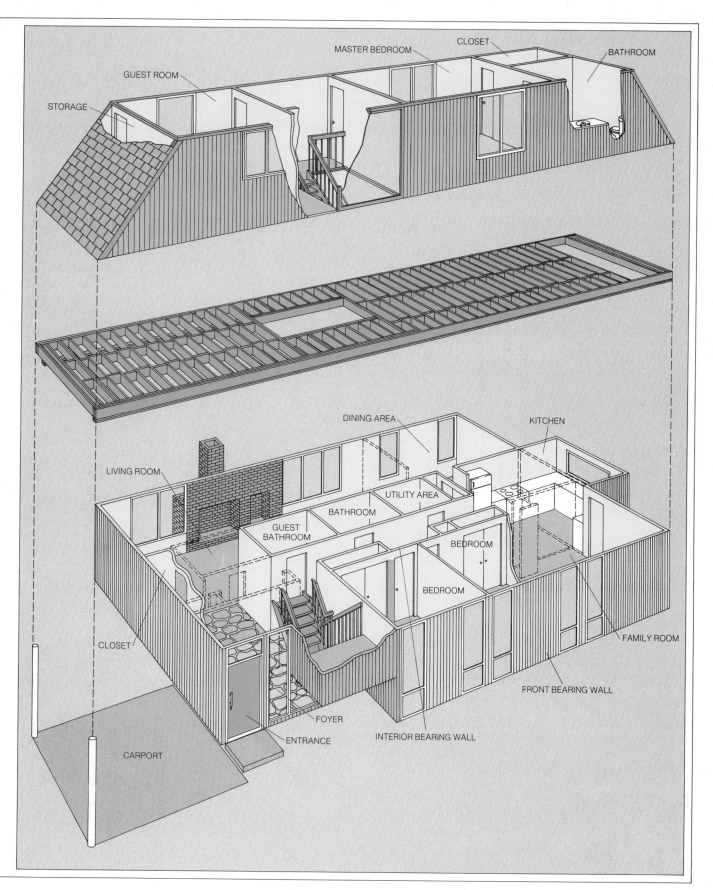

STORAGE

GUEST ROOM

MASTER BEDROOM

CLOSET

BATHROOM

DINING AREA

KITCHEN

LIVING ROOM

UTILITY AREA

BATHROOM

GUEST
BATHROOM

BEDROOM

BEDROOM

FAMILY ROOM

CLOSET

FRONT BEARING WALL

FOYER

ENTRANCE

INTERIOR BEARING WALL

CARPORT

Acknowledgments

The index/glossary for this book was prepared by Louise Hedberg. The editors also wish to thank the following: Charles Alexander, Fort McHenry Lumber Company, Inc., Baltimore, Md.; Joseph Allen, William Gheen and Bernie Pikulski, WACO Scaffold and Shoring Company, Beltsville, Md.; Arel A. Atwell, Alexandria, Va.; Oscar Baughen, Arlington, Va.; Wayne F. Bengtson, United States League of Savings Associations, Chicago, Ill.; Robert Boras, National Association of Home Builders Research Foundation, Washington, D.C.; Kevin Callaghan, National Concrete and Masonry Association, Herndon, Va.; Joseph Chopp and Ken Willis, Brandt and Chopp Roof Truss Company, Brandywine, Md.; George Courville, U.S. Department of Energy, Washington, D.C.; Charles Crocker, Arlington, Va.; Joseph F. Cuba, American Society of Heating, Refrigeration, and Air Conditioning Engineers, New York, N.Y.; Dale Lumber Company, Falls Church, Va.; Del Ray Rental Center, Alexandria, Va.; Al Dennis, A. E. Dennis and Son, Inc., Alexandria, Va.; Ed Detwiler, Virginia Concrete Company, Inc., Springfield, Va.; Devlin Lumber and Supply Company, Rockville, Md.; John Ellis, Clinton, Md.; John Emrico, Fairfax, Va.; Charles Everly, Martin E. Harp and Larry Hufty, Building Department, City of Alexandria, Va.; Thomas J. Fannon and Sons, Alexandria, Va.; Alan L. Hansen, Washington, D.C.; Jeffrey L. Korns, Capital Lighting and Supply, Inc., Alexandria, Va.; Ellen Lovell and Sharon Stark, Credit Union National Association, Madison, Wis.; Bill Lowe, Building Department, County of Fairfax, Va.; David Lustig, Washington, D.C.; Richard L. D. Morris, Department of Family Economics, Kansas State University, Manhattan, Kans.; Jeanette Morrow, Alexandria, Va.; Frank Murphy, Gaddy Construction Company, Burke, Va.; Jim Pierce, Structural Systems, Inc., Gaithersburg, Md.; J. F. Richardson, International Masonry Institute, Washington, D.C.; Robert Ross, Hydronics Institute, Berkeley Heights, N.J.; Jerry Ruka, Tjernlond Products, Inc., St. Paul, Minn.; Frederick W. Sachs, W. A. Smoot and Company, Alexandria, Va.; Chris R. Sheridan, Macon, Ga.; Kenneth Toombs, Smitty's Lumberteria, Alexandria, Va.; Robert Wagner, Electrical Department, County of Arlington, Va.; Steven D. Wesley, Washington, D.C.; Laura Beth, Robert and Steven Yergovich, Alexandria, Va.

Picture Credits

The sources for the illustrations in this book are shown below. The drawings were created by Jack Arthur, Roger C. Essley, Fred Holz, Columbus Knox from B-C Graphics, Joan McGurren and Bill McWilliams. Credits for the pictures from left to right are separated by semicolons, from top to bottom by dashes.

Cover: Fil Hunter. 6: Stephen R. Brown. 9 through 17: Frederic F. Bigio from B-C Graphics. 20: Stephen R. Brown. 22 through 35: Walter Hilmers Jr. 36 through 41: Ray Skibinski. 42 through 48: John Massey. 49: D. Craig Johns. 50: Bradley Olman—Bradley Olman, Erwin Ladau, Architect. 51: Bradley Olman, David Glaser, Architect (2). 52: John Neubauer. 53: John Neubauer, Norman D. Askins, Architect (2). 54: John Neubauer—John Neubauer, Patrick Collins, Architect. 55: John Neubauer, Joanne Goldfarb, Architect. 57 through 65: Frederic F. Bigio from B-C Graphics. 66 through 69. Ray Skibinski. 70 through 75: Forte, Inc. 76 through 79: Whitman Studio, Inc. 80: Stephen R. Brown. 82 through 91: Peter McGinn. 93 through 99: John Massey. 100 through 109: Eduino Pereira. 110: Stephen R. Brown. 112,113: Walter Hilmers Jr. 114 through 117: Frederic F. Bigio from B-C Graphics. 118,119: Eduino Pereira. 120 through 125: Whitman Studio, Inc. 126 through 131: John Massey. 133: Walter Hilmers Jr.

Index/Glossary

Included in this index are definitions of many of the technical terms used in this book. Page references in italics indicate an illustration of the subject mentioned.

Additions, building and constructing: bay window, 8, 9, 20, 21, 22-35, 53; full second story, 14, 15, 132-133; ground-floor additions, 8, 10-11, 21; major additions, 8, 14-15, 111, 112-113; one-story, 10, 11, 36, 56, 66; room above garage, 12, 13, 81, 92-99; second-story additions, 12-13; shed dormer, 12, 51, 81, 82-91; stairs, exterior, 104-109; stairs, interior, 100-103; two-story wing, 14, 15, 111, 112-113; See also Foundation; Roof; Siding; Walls; Window

Additions, preliminary considerations: architectural styles, 7, 8, 9-15, 49-55 (examples), 56; estimating costs, 16-18, 111; financing, 16-18; hiring contractor, 8, 16-17, 18, 19, 76; inspection checklist, 19; planning, 7, 8, 16-17, 18, 19, 21; preparing drawings, 8, 16, 17; property values, 8, 111; soliciting bids, 16, 17, 18

Architect, hiring, 7, 8, 16, 17, 56

Balloon frame: *type of construction in which wall studs run uninterrupted from foundation to rafters, not from floor to floor.* And bay window, 22, 23, 24, 25, 28, 30-31; identifying, 22; walls, 28, 44

Balustrade: *railing along open side of stairway.* Constructed, 109

Batter boards: *markers used to locate building lines of structure.* In crawl-space foundation, 37, 38

Bay window: and balloon frame, 22, 30-31; foundation, 22; framing wall opening, 28-31; header, 28, 29; installation, 22-35; joists, 24-27; and platform frame, 22; prefabricated window unit, 9, 20, 21, 22, 32-33; styles of, 8, 9, 21, 22, 53; roof, 9, 22, 34-35

Blueprint, 17. See also Plans

Brick-veneer walls: and crawl-space foundation, 36, 37, 38; cutting for bay window, 23

Building codes, 12, 19, 36, 66, 92, 96, 104, 107, 112, 114, 115, 120, 124, 125

Carriages: *notched boards that support treads and risers on stairway.* Cutting, 101; described, 100, 104; installing, 102, 107-109

Circuit breaker, installing, 75

Contractor, hiring, 8, 16-17, 18, 19, 76

Cornice: *portion of roof that overhangs the walls.* Box, 57; close, 57; matching old roof, 56, 61; removing, 43

Dormer, shed: *an added attic room with a shed-type roof.* Building, 83-91; described, 7, 12, 51, 81, 82, 83; planning, 82; plumbing for, 120, 125

Drip edge: *metal strip on roof edge to divert rain water.* Installing, 57, 65

Eave: *lower horizontal edge of a roof.* Blending new and old, 56; and box cornice, 57; and close cornice, 57

Electrical codes, 70, 72

Electricity: calculating power load, 70; connecting electrical devices, 74; extending house circuits, 70; fuse box, 75; grounding boxes, 74; grounding the system, 75; installing circuit breaker, 75; mapping out new circuits, 70; mounting boxes, 71; service panel, 70, 71, 72, 73, 75; supplying power to addition, 70-75, 112; wiring addition, 72-73

Elevation view: *drawing showing a front view of vertical parts such as a wall or roof.* Planned, 16

Flashing: *metal strips used to waterproof roof joints and seams.* Use, 35, 57, 63, 64-65

Footings: *concrete supports for foundation walls.* In crawl-space foundation, 37-38; in garage conversion, 92, 96-97; for outside stairway, 104, 107-108; setting girders, 92, 110, 115; in slab foundation, 41, 117

Foundation: and bay window, 22; building above existing foundation, 81; of frame house, 36; of ground-floor addition, 36-41; planning, 36; stepped, 36; of two-story addition, 112-113, 114-117

Foundation, crawl-space: and bay window, 22; footings, 37-38; of ground-floor addition, 36-40; and plumbing, 120, 122-124; of two-story addition, 112-113, 114-117; wall, 38-39; wiring, 72

Foundation, masonry: piers that support girders, 36, 110, 112-113, 114, 115; piers that support outdoor stairs, 104, 107-108; in slab foundation, 41; in two-story addition, 112-113

Foundation, slab: and bay window, 22;

construction, 36, 41; slab-on-block, 36, 41; and subflooring, 36; turned-down, 36, 41; in two-story addition, 114, 117; and utilities, 81

Framing: for bay window, 28-31; around openings cut in walls, 28-31, 46; for plumbing, 121; framing sections of new walls, 42-47, 99; shed dormer, 86-89; in stair well, 101-103; in two-story addition, 114, 118-119

Garage conversion: adding second story, 12, 13, 92, 93-99; adding stairs, 81, 92 100-109; installing girder, 92, 95-97; reinforcing ceiling, 92, 94-97

Girder: *horizontal beam of steel or wood that supports joists.* In foundation, 36, 110; in two-car garage, 92, 95-97, 98; in two-story addition, 112-113, 114-117; wooden, 110, 112-113, 115-116, 117

Gutters, 64, 65

Header: *beam that spans top of a door or window opening.* In balloon-frame opening, 30; for flush opening into ground-floor addition, 66-69; sizes required for wall openings, 28; in wall openings, 46, 47

Heating and cooling systems: energy-saving ideas, 21; extending to addition, 76-79; forced-air system, 76, 78-79; hot-water system, 76-78; in two-story addition, 112

Inspection, building, chart 19, 36, 71, 74

Insulation, and bay window, 27; in crawl-space foundation, 40; in ground-floor addition, 21; for new pipes, 124

Insurance: and contractors, 18, 19; homeowner's, 18; loan, 18

Joists: *horizontal boards that support ceilings and floors.* And bay window, 22-27; in crawl-space foundation, 40; and gable roof, 56; in ground-floor addition, 21, 36, 40; in second-story addition, 132-133; and shed roof, 56

Joists, bay, 22, 24-26, 27

Joists, ceiling: and gable roof, 56; and garage conversion, 92, 94; and shed dormer, 81, 90

Joists, floor: in bay window, 22, 24-27; in crawl-space foundation, 40; exposing, 23; in garage, 92, 98; identifying wall structure, 22; in new walls, 45; splicing and extending, 24-27

Joists, truss, 92, 114, 119